Berlitz

SALZBURG

POCKET GUIDE

Walking Eye
mobile app

Discover the world's best destinations with the Insight Guides Walking Eye app, available to download for free in the App Store and Google Play.

The container app provides easy access to fantastic free content on events and activities taking place in your current location or chosen destination, with the possibility of booking, as well as the regularly-updated Insight Guides travel blog: Inspire Me. In addition, you can purchase curated, premium destination guides through the app, which feature local highlights, hotel, bar, restaurant and shopping listings, an A to Z of practical information and more. Or purchase and download Insight Guides eBooks straight to your device.

TOP 10 ATTRACTIONS

FESTUNG HOHENSALZBURG
The fairy-tale castle dominates the city it was built to defend. See page 30.

RESIDENZPLATZ
The most impressive square in the Old Town. See page 36.

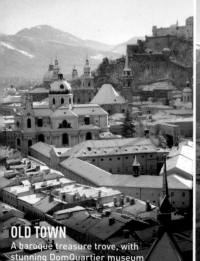

OLD TOWN
A baroque treasure trove, with stunning DomQuartier museum complex. See page 36.

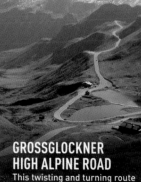

GROSSGLOCKNER HIGH ALPINE ROAD
This twisting and turning route is one of the world's great scenic drives. See page 76.

HELLBRUNN PALACE AND GARDENS
See the grand scale of living of Salzburg's prince archbishops. See page 62.

ST PETER'S ABBEY
The city's spiritual heart and the oldest active monastery in Austria. See page 41.

MOZART'S BIRTHPLACE
The house in which he was born is now a museum. See page 45.

MIRABELL PALACE AND GARDENS
Built for the mistress of an archbishop, here you'll find opulence on a grand scale. See page 57.

KÖNIGSSEE
Take a boat trip across the still waters of this beautiful Bavarian lake not far from Salzburg. See page 71.

MUSEUM OF MODERN ART
This showcase for contemporary art also offers a great view of the city. See page 50.

9.30am

Coffee

Even if you enjoy breakfast at your hotel, a second coffee or tea at the Café Bazar (see page 110) is the Salzburg way to start a day. Many writers have found inspiration in this smart though unpretentious café.

12.15pm

Stunning art

The Museum of Modern Art (closed Mon) must not be missed by art lovers. Its restaurant, m32, is the place for an extravagant lunch break with a superb view from the terrace. Alternatively, descend to town in the Mönchsberg lift and stop at Humboldt Stubn (see page 106) for a traditional midday meal.

2.00pm

Dirndl and Mozartkugel

Getreidegasse (with Mozart's birthplace at No. 9), Judengasse and Goldgasse are shopping heaven. Meander through the lanes and you'll discover top brands in carefully renovated Gothic houses next to old shops selling Dirndl and other local costumes. Tiny Café Fürst (see page 109) at Alter Markt is *the* place to buy the original *Mozartkugel*.

10.30am

The sound of Salzburg

Follow the footsteps of Wolfgang Amadeus Mozart to the Makartplatz, where, at house No. 8, you can climb the stairs to the 18th-century apartment of the Mozart family. Then stroll through Mirabell Gardens, seen in *The Sound of Music*.

11.30am

Invigorating heights

Cross the Salzach at Müllnersteg bridge and head for the pretty Müllner Kirche next to the huge Augustine Brewery. Lovely wooded paths wind south along the top of Mönchsberg, and scenic walking trails lead you down to the Museum of Modern Art.

.15pm

quares and lanes

avour the atmosphere of the cathedral and the
rrounding squares. Stroll from Residenzplatz to
omplatz and then to Kapitelplatz to see the giant
essboard and golden sculpture, *Sphaera*. To the
uth is the cemetery of St Peter, with catacombs
rved into the rock face. Walk up Festungsgasse
e Festungsbahn – funicular train – runs in summer
til 10pm) to Stieglkeller to enjoy a local beer and
anoramic city view.

.30pm

60°

ep into the Salzburg
f 1829 at the Panorama
useum, Residenzplatz
Telescopes reveal
e detail in the 360°
anorama painting
Salzburg and its
rroundings. Then
ead for Mozartplatz and
eep behind the ornate
oors of house No. 4 into
pretty 18th-century
rd with a garden.

9.00pm

High above

Traditional *Gasthäuser*
like Zum Wilden Mann or
Zum Fidelen Affen (New
Town) are cosy places
to enjoy chatty evenings
among locals. To finish
off a day with an exotic
drink and breathtaking
views, the rooftop
terrace lounge of the
Stein Hotel (see page
111) is the place to be.

7.00pm

Keynotes for dinner

The restaurant Triangel (see page 107),on Max
Reinhardt Platz, is a favourite spot of musicians
and singers – and a fine place for dinner. Or savour
authentic Austrian fare at Zipfer Bierhaus (see
page 107) nearby. The Mozart Dinner Concert at
St Peter Stiftskulinarium offers the perfect evening
entertainment for Mozart fans.

CONTENTS

🔵 **INTRODUCTION** 10

🏛 **A BRIEF HISTORY** 14

🎫 **WHERE TO GO** 29

The Mönchsberg and environs 29
The Festung Hohensalzburg 30, Nonnberg convent 33,
Nonntal District – Kai Quarter 35

The Old Town and DomQuartier 36
Residenzplatz 37, The cathedral 39, St Peter's Abbey 41,
Kapitelplatz 42, Mozartplatz 42, Alter Markt 43,
Getreidegasse 44, Festival District 46, Around Gstättengasse 49,
Museum of Modern Art 50, Mülln 51

The New Town 52
Linzergasse 52, St Sebastian's Church 52, Makartplatz 53,
Mirabell Palace and Gardens 57, Kapuzinerberg 59

Salzburg's environs 60
Leopoldskron Lake and Palace 60, Hangar-7 61, Stiegl's
Brauwelt 62, Hellbrunn Palace 62, Klessheim Palace 65

South of Salzburg 67
Untersberg 67, Berchtesgaden 70, Königssee 71, Hallein 72,
Werfen 74, Eisriesenwelt 75, The Grossglockner Road 76,
Krimml Waterfalls 78

The Salzkammergut 79
Fuschlsee 80, Wolfgangsee 81, Mondsee 83

🙂 WHAT TO DO 85

> **Culture and nightlife** 85
> **Shopping** 89
> **Sports** 91
> **Salzburg for children** 94

🍽 EATING OUT 96

🅰 A–Z TRAVEL TIPS 114

🛏 RECOMMENDED HOTELS 136

📖 DICTIONARY 143

📑 INDEX 167

⦿ FEATURES

The Salzburg Card 12
The prince archbishops 16
Mozart in Salzburg 23
Historical landmarks 27
Johann Michael Rottmayr 43
A controversial statue 44
The Stiftung Mozarteum 54
Salzburg and The Sound of Music 56
The Föhn 65
Legends of the Untersberg 68
Winter wonderland 86
Calendar of events 95
Austrian fast food 102

INTRODUCTION

First time visitors to Salzburg are often awed by the consistent dignity and style of the city's baroque architecture. And rarely is a city so delicately worked into a dramatic natural setting. Rising above Salzburg's skyline and visible for kilometres around is the Festung Hohensalzburg, a fortress that sits atop the Mönchsberg mountain and watches over the city.

Below, the Altstadt (Old Town) is dominated by baroque towers and church spires, built by a succession of independent bishops from the 16th to the 18th centuries. This historic centre became a Unesco World Heritage Site in 1996, recognised as an important European ecclesiastical area.

Salzburg is most famous for being the birthplace of Wolfgang Amadeus Mozart and, of course, as the setting for *The Sound of Music*, but the city's wealth of culture extends beyond that. With Easter and Whitsun festivals, as well as Mozart Week in January and the internationally known Salzburg Festival in summer, this is one of the world's top festival cities, vying with Vienna as the cultural capital of Austria. Salzburg also hosts renowned Christmas markets in December, when the city is transformed into a winter wonderland, with ice sculptures, ice rinks, music, stalls and copious amounts of *Glühwein* (mulled wine).

GEOGRAPHY AND CLIMATE

Salzburg is in the west of central Austria and close to the Bavarian border of Germany, in the northern foothills of the Alps. The city lies between two craggy hills, the Mönchsberg and the Kapuzinerberg, and is divided in two by the Salzach River. This was the life-blood of Salzburg for many centuries, used for transporting salt *(Salz)*, gold and copper mined in the mountains, and bringing much wealth to the city during the Middle Ages. Only a few kilometres from the city centre lies the closest real mountain, the Untersberg (1,853m/ 6,078ft).

Salzburg is influenced by the alpine climate, and generally has cold, dry, snowy winters and warm summers with a considerable amount of rain. When it rains here, it really pours. The locals call it *Schnürlregen* – 'string rain'.

Salzburg and the Salzach River

Whatever the season, the weather can be turned on its head by the warm south wind known as the *Föhn* (see page 65).

POLITICS AND RELIGION

Home to approximately 150,000 people, Salzburg is the capital of the province of the same name (pop. 530,000). It is one of Austria's youngest provinces, not incorporated into the country until 1816 (it was previously an independent ecclesiastical state). Austria is a federal state made up of nine provinces, each with its own local government. The Regional Assembly of Salzburg, elected every five years by proportional representation, consists of 36 members who have considerable influence over the politics and economics of the region.

While the role of the church in Salzburg is by no means what it was in the era of prince archbishops, the diocese continues to be one of the most important in the Roman Catholic Church, and the archbishop has direct access to the Pope. The Catholic Church remains a powerful local institution – of the city's 43 churches, 40 of them are Catholic – and owns a lot of land in and around the city, with the final say on where street music, open-air festivals and sporting events can take place. It also has the right to claim a yearly tax from every citizen's salary to help with its upkeep (this tax also extends to other denominations too). Nevertheless, although more than two-thirds of the population counts themselves as Catholic, not many are regular churchgoers.

BEING A SALZBURGER

Salzburgers have a reputation for being aloof, and intimacy is reserved for their own close social circles. They are conservative in nature, though the younger generation is breaking the mould, becoming more outgoing. But this does not reflect the

⊙ THE SALZBURG CARD

A useful money-saver for the serious sightseer is the Salzburg Card, which allows free use of public transport, including the fortress funicular and sightseeing boat, as well as discounts for various cultural events, tours and excursions. It also serves as an admission ticket to the city's most important cultural sights, including Mozart's birthplace, the Hohensalzburg fortress, the DomQuartier Salzburg, the Salzburg Museum and the Museum of Modern Art. Sights outside the town include Hellbrunn Palace, the zoo and the cable-car trip at Untersberg.

Cards are valid for 24, 48 or 72 hours and cost May–Oct €27, €36 or €42, Nov–Apr €24, €32 or €37 – half price for children (6–15 yrs). You can buy the Salzburg Card from hotels, ticket offices and tourist information offices, or visit www.salzburg.info.

whole picture, and citizens are, in general, very friendly towards tourists.

Laws are for obeying in Salzburg: litter is prohibited, jaywalking is not tolerated, crime is almost non-existent and the police operate a zerotolerance policy. This might sound heavy-handed, but walking home at night is usually safe. However, as with most cities, pickpocketing sometimes occurs in crowded places, and you do need to lock up your bicycle.

Downtown Salzburg, near Getreidegasse

Salzburgers enjoy a leisurely pace of life. They do a lot of walking and they frequent coffee houses, beer gardens and taverns to relax. There is no sense of urgency here and certainly not the hectic pace that can be felt in other cities of a similar size.

Salzburg is a university town with a good nightlife scene. The main areas for socialising by night are along Rudolfskai, Gstättengasse and Kaigasse, although there are many taverns scattered throughout the city. The Augustiner Brewery is also a must when visiting the city, with its fine beer halls and huge, tree-lined, summer beer garden.

No matter what time of year you visit Salzburg, there is always something happening, from the street-café way of life in the summer to the Christmas markets in winter. The beauty of the city is enhanced with each season, making Salzburg a perfect year-round destination.

A BRIEF HISTORY

Salzburg's strategic location, near to one of the passes running from north to south through the Alps, brought the city power and prosperity through trade – especially of locally mined salt. But it also brought the city into conflict, as the valley was a major trading route from Italy to Germany.

NEOLITHIC AND CELTIC DEVELOPMENTS

The history of human activity in the Salzburg region can be traced back 6,000 years to the New Stone Age and a settlement on the Rainberg (behind the Mönchsberg). During the Bronze Age, around 1000 BC, the Illyrians settled here, lured by the copper that was mined on the Mitterberg, near Bischofshofen. But in the centuries that followed, salt mining became the primary industry, with mines at Hallstatt and later on the Dürrnberg, near Hallein. By around 500 BC, the Celts had invaded the region and begun to mine salt and to build fortified settlements scattered around the hills. The area became a trading centre and the river was used to transport the salt, a valuable commodity.

ROMAN OCCUPATION

Around 15 BC, the Romans marched into the area, conquered the Celtic kingdom of Noricum and built a road over the Alps to Vivium (today's Klagenfurt). Known as Juvavum, the town acquired the status of a Roman *municipium* in AD 45 and became

Latin inscription

When the foundation for the statue of Mozart, in Mozartplatz, was about to be laid in 1841, a marble floor was uncovered bearing the Latin inscription: 'Here lies happiness. Let no evil enter.'

the seat of one of the largest administrations outside Rome. Its focal point, the Forum, was quite likely to have been situated where Residenzplatz is today. During the reconstruction following World War II, the remains of a huge Roman temple were discovered in the Kaigasse area where the Kasererbräu hotel now stands.

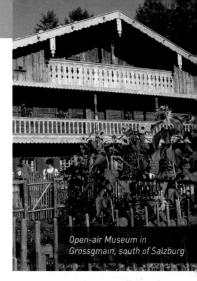
Open-air Museum in Grossgmain, south of Salzburg

Around AD 500, the Baiuvari (Bavarians) laid waste to the city, after the Roman army stationed here had been laid low by an epidemic. They drove out the residents and set Juvavum's wooden structures alight. The ensuing conflagration destroyed most of the settlement, and was the cue for the Romans to withdraw from the province of Noricum.

CHURCH AND STATE COMBINED

Around 696, Bishop Rupert of Worms arrived as a missionary in Bavaria, whose ruler Duke Theodor granted him an area of land, including the remains of Juvavum. Here, Rupert founded the Monastery of St Peter and the Nonnberg Convent. Both institutions remain today, St Peter's as the oldest continuously active monastery in the Roman Catholic Church and the convent as the oldest surviving religious community for women.

Salzburg became a bishopric in 739 and, in the years that followed, one of the most important areas outside the Vatican.

Among the early bishops of note was Virgil, responsible for the town's first cathedral in the mid-8th century. In 798 Salzburg was elevated to the status of an archbishopric by Pope Leo, and Abbot Bishop Arno was promoted to archbishop and a prince of the Holy Roman Empire.

In 996, Emperor Otto III awarded Salzburg a town charter and the right to levy customs duties and mint its own coins. Less

⊙ THE PRINCE ARCHBISHOPS

For more than 1,000 years, Salzburg and its surrounding territories were ruled by prince archbishops: men highly placed in the Holy Roman Empire and wielding great influence. They could depend on the power of the Church to back their causes, commendable or not. And they controlled just about everything: tax collection, land ownership, mining rights, the building of churches, monasteries and places of learning, the armies and, of course, the salvation of souls.

The Church and the state were not separate entities, and the prince archbishop, as the title implies, was at the head of both – usually a head of state first and a religious leader second. The prince archbishop of Salzburg was elected to the position; he was not appointed by the Pope or the Holy Roman Emperor, nor was his position a hereditary title. Indeed, these leaders were not allowed to marry – but that did not stop many of them taking mistresses and having numerous children. Normally, the youngest son of a noble family was nominated for the post.

The prince archbishops displayed varying degrees of benevolence. Many were patrons of the arts, as well as being responsible for the design and development of the city, including the iconic fortress.

than a century later, during the power struggle between the Holy Roman Emperor and the Pope, Archbishop Gebhard of Salzburg weighed in on the side of Pope Gregory II. As protection against the imperial armies, he commissioned the fortresses of Hohensalzburg, Hohenwerfen and Friesach.

The Hohensalzburg fortress

GROWTH AND DESTRUCTION

Under the reign of Konrad I during the 12th century, the Hohensalzburg fortress was developed into a heavily fortified bastion. The high walls that he added can still be seen today.

But the fortress was not able to prevent the events of 1167, when Frederick Barbarossa's troops set fire to the city during a dispute with the Pope (Salzburg sided with the Church), destroying the cathedral. In the years that followed, Salzburg was rebuilt under the direction of Archbishop Konrad III. He also started construction of an immense new cathedral.

By the 13th century, the salt that was mined in Hallein was proving to be increasingly important for the region. The mines produced so much that Salzburg could drop the price considerably, giving the city a trading advantage over the competition from the neighbouring salt mines in Bad Reichenhall and Berchtesgaden. This added to the strength of the Salzburg archbishops who, once they had procured a monopoly on salt trading, were able to raise the prices again.

Although the archbishops had been imperial princes since the 12th century, the areas they ruled were still considered to be part of the Duchy of Bavaria. In the early 14th century, in the machinations between the Bavarian and Austrian royal houses, Archbishop Friedrich III of Salzburg sided with the Austrian Friedrich I ('the Handsome'). Civil war raged for seven years until Louis IV of Bavaria won the decisive battle of Mühldorf in 1322. Although Salzburg had been on the losing side, the result of this internecine strife was that Bavaria was forced to concede its independence. In 1328, Salzburg became an autonomous state, separate from both Bavaria and Austria. However, the city's prosperity was soon to suffer another blow when the plague hit it in 1348, killing around 30 percent of the population.

During the late 14th and early 15th centuries, the traders of Salzburg grew in importance. It was during this period that many of the merchants' houses that survive today in the 'old' and 'new' towns were built. Archbishop Leonhard von Keutschach ruled Salzburg from 1495 to 1519, adding significantly to the size and impregnability of the fortress.

THE PEASANTS' WAR

Keutschach's successor, Matthäus Lang von Wellenberg, exerted political influence far beyond the boundaries of Salzburg. He was a cardinal, a councillor of Emperor Maximilian I and a politician with wide influence. He was decisive in the election of the Medici Pope Clemens VII, and the Habsburg Karl V would never have become emperor without his intervention. But it was on home ground that he faced his sternest challenge.

Salzburg's peasants were restless, suffering from increased taxation and the demands made on them by the nobility and monasteries. Inspired by Martin Luther, they also came to resent the hard line Catholicism and apparent arrogance of their archbishop. In May 1525, they rebelled; the miners of Gastein joined in. The revolt spread beyond the borders of Salzburg, into adjacent Carinthia and Styria, both ruled by the Habsburg dynasty. On 4 June the rebels seized control of Salzburg, and briefly controlled the city as well

Statue of Emperor Maximilian I

as parts of Carinthia, Carniola and Upper Austria. Archbishop Matthäus negotiated an agreement with the rebel leaders, which addressed some of their demands. He promised them a council that would address their grievances, and the peasants broke off their siege of the Hohensalzberg fortress.

But in December 1525, Archbishop Matthäus felt secure enough to act more forcefully. He had a number of rebel leaders arrested and executed. The promised council met in January 1526, but was dissolved without achieving anything. The peasants resumed their revolt, joining forces with the Tyrolean revolutionary Michael Gaismair. But Matthäus, too, had allies, notably the Swabian League, and a force of 10,000 soldiers. There were a number of indecisive battles in May and June 1526, until the rebels were finally defeated at Radstadt.

Matthäus overcame the threat posed by the peasants with a combination of patience, determination, deceit and outside help. Though the Salzburg peasantry continued to lean towards the Lutheran Reformation, Archbishop Matthäus and his successors remained steadfast Catholics, developing a style of absolute rule directed against Salzburg's Protestant elements.

THE CITY TAKES SHAPE

Wolf Dietrich von Raitenau was elected in 1587. He was a man of great vision who began to oversee the architectural design of Salzburg as we know it today, bringing Italian baroque style to the city. He tore down the 'undesirable' areas and in their place built wide, open squares and magnificent residences. Schloss Mirabell was built for his mistress, Salome Alt, who is said to have borne him between 12 and 15 children. His reign came to an end when he quarrelled over mining rights with the prince of Bavaria, whose army attacked Salzburg. Dietrich lost his allies and the support of the Church because of his affair with Salome Alt. Attempting to flee the city, he was captured and imprisoned in the Hohensalzburg fortress, the very building that was designed to protect him.

His nephew and successor was Markus Sittikus. Even though his reign as archbishop lasted only seven years, from 1612 to 1619, Sittikus is credited with continuing the reconstruction of Salzburg that Dietrich had begun, and also instigating new projects such as

Fountain fun

Markus Sittikus is noted for installing the famous water fountains in Hellbrunn Palace. He used to enjoy inviting guests to dinner at the palace and dining outside at the stone table that survives today. He had little water fountains installed in each seat (except his own, of course) and at a given signal, they were turned on, to the discomfort of his guests and the amusement of their host.

the palace and gardens in Hellbrunn. He also laid the foundation stone for the cathedral that dominates Salzburg today.

Sittikus' successor, Paris Graf von Lodron, is acknowledged as Salzburg's greatest prince archbishop. He was elected in 1619 at the start of the Thirty Years' War, the religious battle between Catholics and Protestants. He managed to keep Salzburg out of the dispute, maintaining neu-

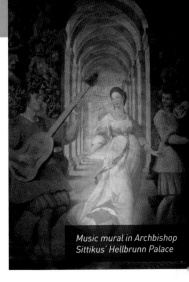

Music mural in Archbishop Sittikus' Hellbrunn Palace

trality and preserving the dominance of the Catholic Church. This was a major achievement as the war left most of Central Europe devastated. During Graf Lodron's 34-year reign, Salzburg's population rose from 40,000 to 80,000. A great believer in education, he founded the university in 1623. He brought new wealth to the city by imposing tolls on traders using the nearby Pass Lueg, and he also expanded the mining and mineral trade of the region. His body was laid to rest beneath the dome of the cathedral.

THE END OF THE PRINCE ARCHBISHOPS

The prince archbishops' dominance over the land of Salzburg ended at the beginning of the 19th century. In 1800, Napoleon defeated the Austrians at the Battle of Marengo and crossed the Alps at the head of a 40,000-strong army, while another French army crossed the Rhine, captured Munich and pushed on to take Linz in Austria. In the years that followed, as the European powers

The most famous Salzburger

challenged Bonaparte on several fronts, Salzburg was bounced around between its larger neighbours.

From 1803 to 1805, Salzburg was an electorate of the Holy Roman Empire of German nations. The religious principality was secularised, and the political authority of the prince archbishops finally came to an end. As part of the 1805 peace treaty of Pressburg, Salzburg was incorporated into Austria. The independent state was now a province of a large empire – but not for long. The Habsburgs declared war on France in 1809, but were defeated. This brought Salzburg under direct French administration for a year and a half. But in 1810, the area as far as the Leuken valley (Kitzbühel) was ceded to Napoleon's ally Bavaria. Salzburg's university was suspended and in 1811 the regional assembly was dissolved.

Following Napoleon's disastrous Russian campaign, Bavaria shrewdly switched its allegiance, and the Salzburgers found themselves once again in opposition to France. By 1814, Napoleon was being attacked on all fronts, and by the end of the year, he had been deposed and banished to Elba. The Great Powers – Austria, Prussia, Russia and Britain – convened the Congress of Vienna, at which the map of Europe was redrawn. Among many other realignments of territories, the Tyrol and Salzburg were assigned to the Habsburg rulers, and in 1816 Salzburg became part of Austria.

⊙ MOZART IN SALZBURG

In 1737, Wolfgang's father Leopold Mozart arrived in Salzburg and enrolled at the university, though shortly afterwards due to his obsession with music he was expelled because he neglected his studies. In 1743, he was accepted into the court orchestra and in 1747 married a local woman, Anna Maria Pertl. The couple had seven children, though only two survived, Maria Anna, known as Nannerl, and Wolfgang Amadeus (christened Joannes Chrysostomus Wolfgangus Theophilus), born in 1756. Leopold began to tutor Nannerl and this eventually became a point of interest and entertainment for young Wolfgang. As Leopold realised his children's talents, he began to spend more time with them, teaching them music with strict discipline and guidance. Mozart excelled at the clavier and was already composing little pieces before the age of five. At six, Mozart accompanied his father on tour, astounding the audiences with his skills. Then, aged only eight, he went to London and performed in front of King George III, dedicating six sonatas to the queen (for which he received 50 guineas). When Mozart played in Italy at the age of 14, the Italians were so amazed by him that they announced the ring on his finger to be a talisman. Obligingly, Mozart removed it and proceeded to play even more beautifully than before.

The prince archbishop at this time was Sigismund von Schrattenbach, who had a genuine interest in music. Sigismund died in 1771 and was succeeded by Archbishop Colloredo, who had little interest in the arts and considered musicians to be among the lowest ranking courtiers. He put an end to the support of the Mozart family, halting their tours, and instead required that they stay in Salzburg and perform to the court. Mozart grew restless and left Salzburg for good at the age of 25.

For the next 100 years, the ruling family left Salzburg to its own destiny, with limited funding and sparse resources to develop the city. The Habsburgs had little interest in residing there and likewise little interest in investing in the city. This turned out to be the saviour of Salzburg's distinctive appearance. Instead of knocking down and reconstructing buildings and infrastructure, there was no other choice than to repair and maintain what today is a vital part of its culture and history.

EARLY 20TH CENTURY

At the beginning of World War I, 49,000 Salzburgers were conscripted into the Austrian army to fight alongside Germany; 6,000 of them were killed and many more taken prisoner. Salzburg itself saw no battles, but the population suffered great hardship because of the lack of supplies. In 1918, the so called 'rucksack war' broke out. Thousands of people, mostly women, set off for the outlying provinces in search of food for their families. Many were caught by the local authorities and charged with black marketeering. At the end of World War I, the Habsburg monarchy was abolished and Austria was declared a republic for the first time, with Salzburg as a *Bundesland*.

In 1920, the first Salzburg Festival opened on the steps of the cathedral with the performance of *Jedermann* (*Everyman*). The festival was founded by many individuals, but notably the theatre director Max Reinhardt, the

Festival founder

Max Reinhardt (1873–1943) was one of the co-founders of the Salzburg Festival. Born in Baden near Vienna in 1873, he was forced into exile in the US in 1938. He was also the founder of the Max Reinhardt Seminar at the University of Vienna, a drama college that runs four-year acting courses.

composer Richard Strauss and Hugo von Hofmannsthal, one of Austria's most renowned poets and lyricists. Its primary aim was to bring great music to the people with little or no influence from commercial contributions. In theory, this aim has been maintained, although today ticket prices range from just affordable to outrageously expensive. The festival was at its height from 1920 to 1938, growing in international stature every year.

Austrian theatre director Max Reinhardt

With the annexation of Austria by Germany in 1938 *(Anschluss)* things changed. Many of the musicians, singers and conductors who had helped make the festival what it was were Jewish or had Jewish relatives. They were not allowed to perform. Before taking over the running of the festival, the Nazi Party accused the Jews and clerics of misusing the festival idea. Max Reinhardt fled the country for England and then the US in 1938. Artur Toscanini, who had conducted many performances prior to the arrival of fascism, had left the country a year previously to conduct in the US. The festival continued in a diminished form with many performances only being held for army personnel until 1944. In 1947, it was relaunched under the patronage of the US Army. The festival flourished once again and was transformed into today's world-famous international music event that takes place every late July and August.

WORLD WAR II AND BEYOND

During World War II, Salzburg again escaped the worst of the horrors. For the first few years of the war, life continued much as it had before. It was only the large number of refugees from bombed cities in Germany that reminded the population that they were at war. But from autumn 1944 to the spring of 1945, a number of American bombing raids took place, killing 547 people.

The Americans were trying to destroy supply lines by targeting the railway tracks, but bombs caused much damage to the old parts of the town, including the cathedral, which suffered a direct hit. In May 1945, American troops entered the city and the war was over for the Salzburgers.

After hostilities ceased, the US Army oversaw Salzburg's post-war reconstruction. In 1955, the occupying troops left Austria and a new republic was declared. There followed a huge amount of construction work; the Festival Halls were built and also many new high-rise buildings and housing estates, so that the city expanded considerably. The university and the cathedral were also rebuilt and, in 1967, a preservation order was placed on the Old Town.

Austria joined the EU in 1995 and the European Monetary Union in 1999. In 2002, the euro replaced the Austrian schilling as the official currency. With the open border between Germany and Austria, the number of tourists visiting Salzburg has increased dramatically. The airport has been enlarged a number of times to cope with the influx of mainly British charter flights. In 1996 the city was placed on the Unesco World Cultural Heritage Site listing, which has attracted yet more visitors. The Salzburg Art Project was started in 2002. Within a decade internationally renowned artists created exceptional sculptures on the main squares of town – including the *Homage to Mozart* by Markus Lüpertz.

HISTORICAL LANDMARKS

4000 BC Stone Age settlement on Rainberg.

1000 BC Illyrian settlement.

500 BC The Celts invade the region and settle; salt mining begins.

15 BC The Romans conquer the region; Juvavum (Salzburg) emerges.

470 St Severin founds a monastic settlement at Salzburg.

c.500 The Bavarians drive out the Romans.

696 Bishop Rupert of Worms is given the city of Salzburg.

c.700 St Peter's Abbey and Nonnberg Convent are founded by Rupert.

739 Salzburg becomes a bishopric and later an archbishopric.

8th century First cathedral built by St Virgil.

1077 Archbishop Gebhard commissions Hohensalzburg fortress.

1167 Frederick Barbarossa burns the city to the ground.

1348–9 Salzburg is struck by plague; a third of the population dies.

16th–17th century Archbishops Wolf Dietrich von Raitenau, Markus Sittikus and Paris Graf von Lodron give the city its modern-day appearance.

1623 University founded by Archbishop Paris Graf von Lodron.

1756 Wolfgang Amadeus Mozart born at Getreidegasse 9.

1781 Mozart moves to Vienna after arguing with the archbishop.

1800 French troops march into Salzburg.

1816 Salzburg becomes part of the Austro-Hungarian Empire.

1861 First elected parliament and provincial government in Salzburg.

1917 Salzburg Festival Hall Association founded.

1920 Salzburg becomes a province of the Democratic Republic of Austria.

1938 German troops march into Austria.

1945 US troops enter the city.

1956–60 Building of the Large Festival Hall.

1967 Easter Festival founded. Old Town preserved by law.

1996 Old Town of Salzburg becomes a World Cultural Heritage Site.

2006 250th anniversary of Mozart's birth celebrated.

2015 *The Sound of Music* 50th-anniversary celebrations.

2017 Long-time (1999–2017) mayor of Salzburg Heinz Schaden resigns following his involvement in a financial scandal.

The gardens of Mirabell Palace

WHERE TO GO

Although in tourist terms, Salzburg is geared towards everything Mozart, the city also offers a multitude of fascinating historical sights. There are ample churches, graveyards, gardens and alleyways dating back to medieval times. Salzburg is divided into an Old Town and a New Town, on opposite sides of the Salzach, and this chapter has been divided into areas of interest on both sides of the river, followed by a number of excursions. Depending on how much time you have, a walking tour is recommended to fully appreciate all that Salzburg has to offer (see page 125). As the exact opening times for some of the sights vary from year to year, you might want to check with the Tourist Information Office on Mozartplatz on arrival.

For the sights such as the zoo, the Untersberg and Hellbrunn Palace, you can take a bus from the railway station or Hanuschplatz. Hallein and Werfen can be reached by train from the railway station. A bus will take you to the Salzkammergut lake district (see page 79), but the area is better appreciated if you hire a car. You can also visit the Grossglockner High Alpine Road and the Krimml Waterfalls by car or on an organised excursion.

THE MÖNCHSBERG AND ENVIRONS

The great Mönchsberg rock which towers over the Old Town provides Salzburg with a spectacular backdrop of white cliffs. Some of the earliest people in the area settled on this mountain as it provided a natural defence against predators and invaders from nearby territories. A walk across the Mönchsberg's ridge, strewn with old battlements, crumbling walls and contemporary sculptures, provides today's visitors with panoramic and tree-framed views of Salzburg and is an excellent introduction to the city's main sights. Below the eastern ridge is the Old Town, with the impressive baroque museum complex of DomQuartier Salzburg. Further to the northeast, across the Salzach River, is the New Town, built in the shadow of the Kapuzinerberg.

As well as the funicular train on Festungsgasse, there are many routes up the Mönchsberg if you don't mind quite a steep uphill walk. A lift on Gstättengasse allows easy access to the Museum of Modern Art (see page 50).

THE FESTUNG HOHENSALZBURG

On top of the Mönchsberg sits the magnificent fortress, the **Festung Hohensalzburg ❶** (tel: 8424 3011; www.salzburg-burgen.

Hohensalzburg fortress

at/en/hohensalzburg;
daily Jan–Apr and Oct–Dec
9.30am–5pm, May–Sept
9am–7pm, Easter and
weekends in Dec 9.30am–
6pm, last entry 30 mins
prior to closing; basic
ticket includes the funicular to the fortress, access
to the external parts of
the fortress as well as
to the interior area with
an audio-guide tour, all
the museums and Alm
Passage, standard ticket
also includes the prince's

The view from the fortress

apartments and the Mechanical Theatre).

The Hohensalzburg is the largest and best-preserved
fortress in Europe, its dominating bastions, walls and towers making it the symbol of Salzburg. It has had a fascinating history under its many ruling archbishops. Construction
began in 1077 under the reign of Archbishop Gebhard and it
was enlarged and renovated up until the 17th century. Its late
Gothic appearance is largely due to the building work of archbishop Leonhard von Keutschach, who ruled from 1495 to 1519
and was not only a religious leader but also, like many archbishops, a powerful temporal ruler. He thus needed constant
protection from outside invasion and even revolts from within
his own territories. During this period, the main building of the
fortress was significantly enlarged. There is a marble memorial to von Keutschach on the wall of St George's Church, and
he is also commemorated by numerous insignia and coats

of arms that include his curious personal symbol, the turnip, which was staple food in Europe before the introduction of potatoes. Since von Keutschach's time, the lion that is the symbol of the fortress has held a turnip in its paws.

The Hohensalzburg was more than just a defensive fortress and residence in war-torn times. During periods when there was no direct military threat to the city, it was used as a barracks and a prison. Archbishop Wolf Dietrich von Raitenau was held prisoner there by his nephew and successor, Markus Sittikus, for five years until his death in 1617.

The rich and lavishly decorated interior of the fortress is a breathtaking display of intricate Gothic wood carvings and ornamental paintings. Two rooms not to be missed are the **Golden Chamber**, which features stunning detailed wood ornamentation and a majolica ceramic oven from the 1500s, and the **Golden Hall**, with its magnificent wood panelling and carving, and a fascinating ceiling supported by large twisted pillars.

One unique exhibit is the **Salzburger Stier** (Salzburg Bull), possibly the oldest working barrel organ in the world, built in 1502 and lovingly restored, which roars out melodies by Mozart and Haydn.

The fortress contains no less than three museums,

Hangman's House

which span a variety of topics and can only be seen after an officially conducted tour of the fortress. The **Rainer-Regiments-Museum** (www.rainer-regimentsmuseum-salzburg.at) is full of military paraphernalia recalling the Imperial and Royal Regiment of Archduke Rainer; the modern **Fortress Museum** (www.salzburgmuseum.at) has medieval art, weapons, instruments of torture and a variety of everyday objects that illuminate the

Hangman's House

If you take the fortress tour up to the Reck watchtower, you will be rewarded with a spectacular view of the city and beyond. The white house in the middle of the open green space to the southwest is known as the Hangman's House. It is said that such was the desire of the citizens not to live next to the city's hangman that he was obliged to live alone in this isolated location.

history of the fortress and its occupants. The **Marionettenmuseum** in the cellars of the fortress captures the spirit of the famous Salzburg Marionette Theatre with a display of historical puppets.

Even if you're not particularly interested in ancient fortresses, Hohensalzburg is worth a visit just for the views. From the Reck watchtower you get a panoramic sweep of the Alps, and the Kuenburg bastion offers a fine view of Salzburg's domes and towers.

NONNBERG CONVENT

On the southeastern side of the Mönchsberg, to the east of the Hohensalzburg Fortress, is the **Nonnberg Benedictine Convent ❷** (daily 7am–dusk; closed during Mass), which is the oldest convent in the German-speaking world. As with many

Cemetery at St Peter's church

buildings in Salzburg, fire destroyed the original and what we see today is a Gothic-style convent from the 1400s, though extensive renovations were carried out in 1895 and 1951. It is full of interesting artefacts, though visitors are only allowed into the church and St John's Chapel.

The convent was founded in *c*.712 by St Rupert, who promptly appointed his niece, St Erentrudis, as the first abbess. The founding patron of the Romanesque church, Henry II, built a basilica here in 1009, and the 12th-century frescoes are some of the most impressive wall paintings in Austria. The church was severely damaged by fire in 1423. In 1464, the abbess, Agatha von Haunsberg, began the reconstruction in a Gothic style, creating the unique crypt and the magnificent reticulate rib-vaulting. The tomb of St Erentrudis is located in the apse and most of the frescoes are from the 12th century. There is also a tombstone for Maria Salome, daughter of Archbishop Wolf Dietrich and his mistress, Salome Alt. In the nuns' choir there is a winged altar with a central shrine revealing the Madonna between the two patron saints, Rupert and Virgil.

St John's Chapel (near the entrance, ask for admittance at the porter's lodge, daily 7am–dusk) features a Gothic-winged altar from the late 1400s. The four figures on the south door pay homage to St Erentrudis, the Virgin Mary, St Rupert and Emperor Henry II.

The Sound of Music footnote: in 1927 the real-life Maria Kutschera and Baron von Trapp were married at Nonnberg Convent. Maria had been a student here in 1924.

NONNTAL DISTRICT – KAI QUARTER

If you walk around the convent building and along the Nonnberggasse you will eventually come out at Brunnhausgasse. Follow this road to the right and you will get to the **Leopoldskron** district (see page 60), while heading left you will shortly reach the quiet **Nonntaler Hauptstrasse**. Situated here is the Erhardplatz, which sits in front of the church of **St Erhard im Nonntal**. Built in 1685 by the architect Johann Caspar Zuccalli, it has a richly decorated interior of stucco and a high altar painting by Johann Michael Rottmayr from 1692.

Below the Nonnberg Convent to the north is **Kajetanerplatz**, whose notable feature is the **Kajetanerkirche St Maximilian ❸**. It was consecrated in 1700 and only properly finished after 1730, based on plans by Johann Zuccalli. The portrait of the Holy Family on the left side altar is by Johann Michael Rottmayr; all the other altar paintings and the ceiling fresco are the work of Paul Troger. The Holy Staircase (1712), to the left of the main body of the church, is based on the Scala Santa in Rome.

Salzburg's signs

Salzburg is full of signs and insignias carved into walls and doorways. If you see 'C+M+B' and a year written in chalk above a door, this means that the carol singers dressed as the Three Wise Men have been to the house around 6 January and received a donation for charity.

Leading off Kajetanerplatz is the quiet shopping street of **Kaigasse**, which is lined with shops, galleries and coffee houses. Most of these buildings were once the homes of priests. On Chiemseegasse, off Kaigasse, is an even more elevated ecclesiastical residence, the **Chiemseehof ❹**. From the 14th century, this was the seat and residence of the bishops of Chiemsee in Bavaria, a filial diocese of Salzburg. The Chiemseehof is not open to visitors, as it now houses the province of Salzburg's regional parliament (Salzburger Landtag) and government (Salzburger Landesregierung).

THE OLD TOWN AND DOMQUARTIER

The **Altstadt** (Old Town) is a combination of tall merchants' houses and narrow alleys, along with the baroque buildings and squares of the Prince-Archbishops' quarter. In 2014, the quarter was transformed into **DomQuartier Salzburg** (Residenzplatz 1; www.domquartier.at; all sights Wed–Mon 10am–5pm, also Tue July–Aug and Dec, Wed until 8pm in July–Aug; combined ticket to all sights), a museum complex centred around baroque art, with over 2,000 exhibits. The main sights it incorporates are: the Residenz State Rooms and Gallery, the Cathedral Museum, North Oratory and Organ Gallery, St Peter Abbey's Museum and Long Gallery and the Cabinet of Curiosities. You can either embark upon a self-guided tour of all or selected sights with an informative audio guide (available in nine languages) or choose from a wide array of guided tours. As well as exploring these museums, visitors can experience places that have been inaccessible to the public for the last 200 years, like the cathedral terrace, linking the Residenz with the cathedral, with its impressive views of Salzburg and the mountains.

RESIDENZPLATZ

The largest square of the Old Town is **Residenzplatz**. It is used for seasonal markets and events, though one stunning constant is the **Residenz Fountain**, created by Tommaso di Garona between 1656 and 1661. The fountain is 15m (50ft) high and is said to be the largest and most beautiful baroque fountain outside Italy. If you are visiting in wintertime, though, you will find it covered up for protection against the elements.

The **Residenz** ❺ was the residence and seat of the prince archbishops. A bishop's residence had existed on this site since medieval times; the present building, an extensive complex enclosing three large courtyards, was built around the turn of the 17th century for Archbishop Wolf Dietrich von Raitenau.

Stiftskirche St Peter

The imposing Residenz Fountain

The marble portal on Residenzplatz leads into the main courtyard which is the entrance to Dom-Quartier. Decorated in late baroque style, the state rooms and apartments of the Residenz feature fine wall and ceiling paintings by Johann Rottmayr and Martino Altomonte. As a member of the Salzburg court music ensemble, the young Mozart would regularly perform before invited guests in the Rittersaal (Knights' Hall), which is still used as a concert venue today. On the third floor is the **Residenz Gallery**, where European paintings from the 16th to the 19th century are displayed.

East of the fountain is the **Neue Residenz** (New Residence), built by Archbishop Wolf Dietrich as a 'guest wing'. In 1695, the famous **Glockenspiel** was added by Prince Archbishop Johann Ernst Graf Thun. Each day at 7am, 11am and 6pm the 35 bells ring out across the city, with the tunes changing according to the season (www.salzburgmuseum.at; guided tours end-Mar–Oct Thu 5.30pm, Fri 10.30am).

The Neue Residenz is home to the **Salzburg Museum** ❻ (entrance on Mozartplatz; www.salzburgmuseum.at; Tue–Sun 9am–5pm). The collection features art and artefacts from all periods of Salzburg's history, ranging from prehistoric objects, such as a Celtic beaked pitcher and a Bronze-Age helmet, to a set of early 19th-century Romantic paintings of the city. The

Rossacher Collection of baroque designs, sketches and boz-
zetti (sculptors' initial models of their planned creations) was
moved here in 2012 from the Baroque Museum, which has
now been incorporated into the Salzburg Museum. Parts of
the collection are presented at the North Oratory of Salzburg
Cathedral which is part of DomQuartier. The **Panorama
Museum** (entrance at Residenzplatz; www.salzburgmuseum.
at; daily 9am–5pm) shows the fascinating panorama painting (26m/85ft long) of Salzburg and its surroundings by J.M.
Sattler, documenting life in Salzburg around 1829.

THE CATHEDRAL

Leaving Residenzplatz through the archways will bring you
onto the **Domplatz**, home to **Salzburg's Cathedral** ❼ (May–
Sept Mon–Sat 8am–7pm, Sun and hols 1–7pm, Jan–Feb and
Nov until 5pm, Mar–Apr, Oct and Dec until 6pm; donation
required). In the centre of the square is the statue of the Virgin
Mary, a masterpiece of the Hagenauer brothers, created in
1766. Each year the opening of the Salzburg Festival is celebrated here with a performance of *Jedermann (Everyman)*.

The cathedral, the most impressive baroque edifice north of
the Alps, is the ecclesiastical centre of Salzburg. The original
cathedral on this site was built by Bishop Virgil in 767. It was
destroyed by fire in 1167, and ten years later a new cathedral
was built on a grander scale, only to be destroyed once again
by fire in 1598. The then archbishop, Wolf Dietrich, demolished
the remains and dug up the graveyard in order to start rebuilding from scratch. But his plans were never realised as he was
imprisoned by his nephew and successor, Markus Sittikus, who
commissioned Santino Solari to rebuild the cathedral to a different design. The building escaped damage during the Thirty Years'
War and was consecrated with much pomp and ceremony. Much

Salzburg's cathedral

later, it suffered a third calamity during a bombing raid in 1944, when the dome was destroyed. The cathedral was re-consecrated in 1959 after renovations. At the gates of the cathedral you can see the dates of the three consecrations: 774, 1628 and 1959. The towering white statues at the cathedral gates depict the patron saints Rupert and Virgil (outside) and the two apostles Peter and Paul (inside).

The cathedral's interior dates mostly from the 17th century. The only earlier survival is the 1321 font, supported by four even older 12th-century lions, where Mozart was baptised. One of the most impressive items in the cathedral is the massive and majestic organ, which is guarded by carved angels.

In the cathedral's magnificent baroque oratories is the **Cathedral Museum**, part of DomQuartier (www.domquartier. at), which displays artefacts spanning its 1,300-year history, including medieval sculptures, baroque paintings and gold articles from the cathedral treasury. The oldest exhibit is St Rupert's 8th-century crozier.

The Cathedral Excavations Museum (www.salzburgmuseum. at; July–Aug daily 9am–5pm), revealing ruins of the original Romanesque cathedral foundations, above-ground wall sections and excavations from a Roman villa, is entered around the corner on Residenzplatz, left of the main entrance (see page 37).

ST PETER'S ABBEY

Below the Hohensalzburg fortress, at the foot of the Mönch-sberg, is the peaceful complex of **Stiftskirche St Peter (St Peter's Abbey) ❽**, the oldest active monastery in Austria and part of DomQuartier Salzburg. Founded in c.696 by St Rupert, a Frankish missionary, St Peter's is recognised as the spiritual centre around which Salzburg grew. Having been destroyed by fire in 1127 and thereafter subjected to many alterations, the church shows traces of several architectural styles. Its Romanesque tower, for instance, is topped by a baroque cupola. Similarly, the interior is high Romanesque, but the altars are definitively in the rococo style. Most of the altar paintings are by Martin Johann Schmidt, and show his charac-teristic style with its contrasts of light and dark. There is also a plaque dedicated to Nannerl, Mozart's sister, and a memorial to the composer Johann Michael Haydn, the younger brother of the more famous Franz Joseph.

St Peter's bore witness to the music of 13-year-old Mozart in 1769: he wrote his *Dominicus Mass* (K66) for the first Mass offi-ciated here by his childhood friend Kajetan Rupert Hagenauer, later the abbot of St Peter's. In 1783, Mozart's *Mass in C Minor* (K427) was first performed here under the direction of the com-poser, with his new wife Constanze singing the soprano part.

The church's **cemetery** is sprinkled with beautiful wrought-iron grave markers. This is the final resting place of many of Salzburg's aristocracy, and also of Nannerl Mozart, who died in October 1829. Bordering the cemetery are the famous **catacombs** (daily May–Sept 10am–6pm, Oct–Apr 10am–5pm). These were carved into the wall of the rock during early Christian times and emanate a spiritual eeriness.

On the right, next to the church, is Stiftskulinarium St Peter (daily 11.30am–11pm), a wine tavern since 803 and nowadays

Ornate gravestone in St Peter's cemetery

a traditional restaurant complex where you can enjoy the finest *Salzburger Nockerl* in town (see page 97) and the fantastic Mozart Dinner Concert (see page 89).

KAPITELPLATZ

If you leave St Peter's by the cemetery exit, you will find yourself in **Kapitelplatz**, which is easily recognisable by the massive chessboard on the ground – right next to the stunning contemporary sculpture *Sphaera* (2007) by the German sculptor Stephan Balkenhol. The male figure on the golden shimmering sphere is the counterpart to Balkenhol's *Woman in the Rock*, inserted in the rock face on Toscaninihof (west of St Peter's). Also on Kapitelplatz is **Neptune's Fountain**, built in 1732 by the sculptor Anton Pfaffinger on the site of one of the old horse ponds. During the summer months, Kapitelplatz is host to markets, sports events and many artists and musicians. On the far south side of the square, you will find the entrance to the Festungsgasse, which is the road up to the fortress and the **Stieglkeller** (mid-Apr–Dec daily 11am–11pm, early Jan–mid-Apr Wed–Sun only), a classic brewery pub offering good beer, food and a stunning panorama.

MOZARTPLATZ

Walking from Kapitelplatz back to Residenzplatz and passing the Salzburg Museum brings you to **Mozartplatz**, a square dominated by a statue of Salzburg's favourite son. The disappointingly small bronze statue of Mozart was unveiled on 5 September 1842 as the composer's two sons looked on. His widow Constanze had died in March of that year, and at Mozartplatz No. 8 you will find a plaque dedicated to her memory. The statue, originally scheduled to be unveiled in 1841, had been delayed for a year because a Roman mosaic floor was discovered on the site during the preparations for its installation.

ALTER MARKT

There are two main exits leading off Mozartplatz. To the east is Kaigasse, the main street in the old Kai Quarter (see page 35). To the west is **Judengasse**, home to the Jews of Salzburg until they were expelled from the city in 1498. This cobbled pedestrian street scores highly for charm and unusual shops, including a Christmas Shop, where you can buy yuletide decorations all year round, and a shop selling beautifully decorated eggs for use as Easter decorations.

⊙ JOHANN MICHAEL ROTTMAYR

Johann Michael Rottmayr (1654–1730) was a renowned baroque artist, born in Laufen, Salzburg Province, whose style was influenced by the Venetian art of painting in the 16th century. His speciality was ceiling frescoes – he designed and executed most of those in the Salzburg Residenz and also in the Viennese Winter Riding School. He designed the altar in the Universitätskirche in Salzburg and the original painting *The Apotheosis of St Charles Borromeo* (the intercessor for people stricken with the plague), which can be seen in the Residenz Gallery.

Judengasse ends as you reach **Alter Markt ❾**, another of Salzburg's busy squares. Besides the impressive fountain that surrounds a statue of St Florian, you will also find the chemist, Hofapotheke, the oldest in Salzburg and still displaying its medicinal preparations in old brown vials. Just opposite the chemist, at No. 10A, is the smallest shop in Salzburg, formerly a residence. If you are thirsty at this stage, have a coffee in Café Tomaselli, which has been in the Alter Markt since 1705.

GETREIDEGASSE

Leading on from Judengasse, west of Alter Markt, is Salzburg's most famous shopping street, **Getreidegasse ❿**. Whether you like shopping or not, you should have at least one walk down this busy pedestrian street. One of the first things you will notice are the skilfully crafted wrought-iron guild signs that

⦿ A CONTROVERSIAL STATUE

Right from the start, the statue of Mozart in Mozartplatz has been the cause of controversy. Intended to commemorate the 50th anniversary of Mozart's death, the statue was eventually unveiled a year late, at the 51st anniversary. As part of the unveiling ceremony, Mozart's son, a minor composer and musician, performed only a few of his father's works before moving on to play some of his own compositions. He was soon dismissed from the stage.

As for the statue itself, by all accounts it is not a very good likeness. And it includes a glaring anachronism. The composer is portrayed holding a pencil in his hand, even though pencils were not invented until 20 or 30 years after his death. Mozart would have written with a quill pen.

hang above most of the shops and give the street its special character. Also of interest are the numerous passageways and courtyards leading off the Getreidegasse, notably the Schatz-Haus-Passage which has an impressive relief of the Madonna and Child and enters onto Universitätsplatz. Looking up you may notice that as the houses get taller, their windows get smaller, creating a strange optical

Mozart statue in Mozartplatz

effect. There are shops here selling traditional Dirndl (women's dresses) and *Loden* clothes (made of felt-like woollen cloth) and others offering authentic Austrian food.

The Getreidegasse is also part of the pilgrimage trail for Mozart fans: No. 9 is **Mozart's Birthplace** ⓫, the house where he was born on 27 January 1756 and lived with his family until 1773. The Mozarts' apartment on the third floor and the rooms on the second floor have been transformed by Robert Wilson into a slick museum (www.mozarteum.at; daily Sept–June 9am–5.30pm, July–Aug 8.30am–7pm; last entry 30 mins prior to closing). On display are manuscripts (facsimiles), documents and souvenirs, and portraits of the family members, including *Mozart at the Piano*, an unfinished 1789 oil painting by Wolfgang's brother-in-law, Joseph Lange. Also here are instruments that were played by the great musician: his concert piano and clavichord, his concert and child's violin, and a viola.

All of the passageways leading off Getreidegasse to the south reach Universitätsplatz (University Square), which is home to the academic district and the **Kollegienkirche** (Collegiate Church) **12** (daily 9am–6pm; free), one of Johann Bernhard Fischer von Erlach's finest achievements. The interior is immensely high and features an array of angels on stucco clouds surrounding the Madonna. Universitätsplatz is the site of the daily vegetable market, which can be rather expensive.

FESTIVAL DISTRICT

Just east of here on Herbert-von-Karajan-Platz is the picturesque **Pferdeschwemme** (Horse Pond and Fountain), which incorporates a stunning mural of horses. The fountain was built in 1695 to serve as the washing area for the prince archbishops' horses that were kept in stables next door.

Horse Pond and Fountain

These stables along Hofstallgasse have latterly been occupied by the famous **Festspielhäuser** **13** (Festival Halls; www.salzburgerfestspiele.at; guided tours daily July–Aug 9.30am, 2pm and 3.30pm, Sept–June 2pm). This is where, each year in high summer, Salzburg plays host to one of the best-known music

festivals in the world, the Salzburger Festspiele. The festival is centred on the three main venues here, though other locations around the city are also used. Based around the old Riding School, which was built in 1693 to train the archbishop's cavalry, the present Festival Halls still preserve the original façade of the baroque horse stables. Nowadays, the **Felsenreitschule** (Riding School) is a theatre with a retractable roof for open-air performances, hosting high-calibre operas and dramas. Next to the Felsenreitschule is the **House for Mozart**. This, the former Small Festival Hall, has been completely rebuilt with dramatically increased capacity. Adjoining the Felsenreitschule on its other flank is the 2,177-seat **Grosses Festspielhaus** (Large Festival Hall), designed by the Austrian architect Clemens Holzmeister (built 1956 to 1960) and inaugurated by the conductor Herbert von Karajan. Guided tours – the only way to see the

Altar in the Franciscan Church

Festival Halls unless you attend a concert – provide a fascinating insight into the world of theatre.

The eastern end of Hofstallgasse opens into Max-Reinhardt-Platz, where the **Rupertinum** (www.museumdermoderne.at; Tue and Thu–Sun 10am–6pm, Wed until 8pm) houses an important art collection of 20th-century works, with changing exhibitions. It is part of the Museum der Moderne Salzburg (Museum of Modern Art), with the main exhibition high up on Mönchsberg (see page 50).

East of the Rupertinum is Sigmund-Haffner-Gasse, where you will find the entrance to the **Franziskanerkirche** (Franciscan Church) ⑭ (daily 6.30am–7.30pm; closed during Mass), an elegant combination of baroque, Romanesque and Gothic styles. A church was originally built here in the 8th century, but the city fire of 1167 destroyed all but the nave. Rebuilding around this core soon commenced and the building was consecrated in 1223. More additions followed, and the church was finally completed in 1460 by Stephan Krumenauer. Originally part of St Peter's Abbey, it was handed over to the Franciscans by Archbishop Wolf Dietrich. Definitely worth a look is the high altar by Johann Bernhard Fischer von Erlach and the Gothic statue of the Virgin Mary by Michael Pacher.

In the court Dietrichsruh just north of the church, the sculpture *AWILDA* (2010), the 5m-high (16ft) head of a young woman, by the contemporary Catalan artist Jaume Plensa, contrasts with the baroque architecture of the university buildings.

AROUND GSTÄTTENGASSE

At the northeastern side of the Mönchsberg (see page 29) is the **Gstättengasse**, where old houses are snugly built into the rock of the hill. In 1669, a rockfall killed 220 people, which is why there are rock cleaners whose job it is to scale the vertical rocks after the snow has melted to chip away at any loose stones or potential hazards.

At the northern end of Gstättengasse is another **Mozart statue ⑮**, Markus Lüpertz's controversial sculpture *Homage to Mozart*. It was erected in 2005 in anticipation of the 250th anniversary of Mozart's birth the following year and lends a modern touch to **Ursulinenplatz**. The former Ursuline Chapel is now called **St Mark's Church** (Markuskirche). After the original chapel was destroyed by the 1669 rockfall, it was rebuilt and completed in 1705 by the architect Johann Bernhard Fischer von Erlach, who had to accommodate his design to suit the complicated wedge shape of the site.

Around the corner at Museumsplatz is the **Haus der Natur ⑯**, Salzburg's modern Museum of Natural Science and Technology (www.hausdernatur.at; daily 9am–5pm). As well as the usual stuffed specimens, it has an impressive collection of live reptiles and a 36-tank aquarium. Besides wildlife, there are also mineral and geology displays and the Space Research Hall, with a life-size diorama of man's first steps on the moon. The museum also stages exhibitions and has a lovely terrace café. Just past the southern end of Gstättengasse is the **Church of St Blasius**, one of the oldest Gothic hall churches

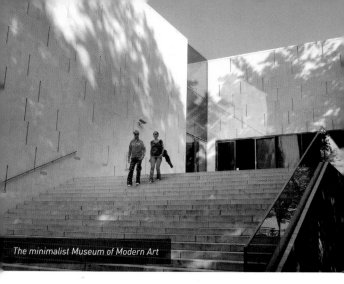

The minimalist Museum of Modern Art

in existence (1330–50). The former civic hospital adjacent houses the **Spielzeugmuseum** ⓱ (Toy Museum; www.salzburg museum.at; Tue–Sun 9am–5pm). Displayed here are all kinds of old toys – such as dolls' houses, miniature trains and railways, optical illusions, musical instruments and paper theatres – giving a fascinating insight into the childhood pleasures of times past. The colourful interactive exhibition has very different play areas – be it with teddy bears or wooden tools to construct big cranes. This is fun for the whole family, starting with free felt slippers to feel at home right from the beginning.

MUSEUM OF MODERN ART

A lift at Gstättengasse 13 allows access to the top of the Mönchsberg, where you will find the **Museum der Moderne** ⓲ (Museum of Modern Art; www.museumdermoderne.at; Tue and Thu–Sun 10am–6pm, Wed until 8pm). Straight lines, shimmering glass and bright white stone create a stark minimalist edifice, which dominates the northwestern ridge of the Mönchsberg, 60m (200ft) above the shores of the Salzach. Built on the site of the old Café Winkler, which crowned the plateau for many decades, the building, designed by the Munich architects team Friedrich Hoff Zwink, opened in 2004. It respectfully incorporates the old tower into its new structure. The four levels, clad with bright white Untersberg marble, are designed to accommodate an ever-changing and diverse range of exhibitions, plus permanent collections. The glass ceilings and the use of stairways as natural light shafts add to the viewing pleasure. If you are feeling peckish and have some cash to spare, then try out the m32 restaurant, which offers one of the best panoramic views of the city. The museum can also be reached by walking along the Mönchsberg from the fortress (see page 30). Close to the museum you also find some contemporary sculptures, including *Numbers in the Woods* by Mario Merz, forming part of the Salzburg Art Project 2002–2011. From 2002 to 2011 a different international artist was invited annually to execute a work in a public space, turning Salzburg into an outdoor sculpture park.

MÜLLN

North of the Mönchsberg is the **Mülln** district of Salzburg. This neighbourhood is home to a celebrated brewery run by monks, **Augustinerbräu** ⑲ (www.augustinerbier.at; Mon–Fri 3–11pm, Sat–Sun 2.30–11pm). Visitors can enjoy the strong brown ale in a grand and delightfully traditional tavern, where the large beer garden is a great place to meet locals and tourists during the summer months.

The brewery and tavern at the **Mülln Monastery** have been in existence since 1621, hence the unique taste of the beer, which is brewed using traditional, old-fashioned methods. The monastery, built on the northern slopes of the Mönchsberg between 1607 and 1614, was founded by monks of the Augustine order, who were called to Salzburg from Bavaria by Archbishop Wolf Dietrich. When the monks began to dwindle in number during the 19th century, the monastery was handed over to the Benedictines from Michaelbeuern. It is now the parish church of Mülln. The interior dates from 1738 and has magnificent examples of delicate baroque detail.

THE NEW TOWN

LINZERGASSE

The Staatsbrücke (State Bridge) over the Salzach leads to the new side of town – though it's only new in comparison with its ancient counterpart across the river. Walking directly over the bridge you will reach **Linzergasse ⑳**, which brims with historical sights and stories. Many of the old houses were built during the 14th and 15th centuries, though a devastating fire in 1818 caused serious damage to the north side of the river. The Linzergasse was rebuilt and several of the old burgher houses were renovated and still line the street today. The house at No. 3 was the residence of the natural scientist Paracelsus (Theophratus Bombastus von Hohenheim), who lived here between 1540 and 1541. On the wall of the Hotel Gablerbräu is a plaque dedicated to the operatic baritone Richard Mayr, born here in 1877.

ST SEBASTIAN'S CHURCH

Just opposite the Gablerbräu is the grand entrance to the climb up the Kapuzinerberg, the hill that dominates the skyline on the north side of town (see page 59). Slightly further up the Linzergasse is the entrance to the **Church of St Sebastian ㉑**.

The original Gothic church was built between 1505 and 1512 by Archbishop Leonhard von Keutschach. Deteriorating over the years, it was torn down in 1750 and replaced with a baroque hall. The town fire of 1818 destroyed parts of the church, most regrettably the ceiling frescoes and high altar painting. The church was renovated again in 1820 (only the 1752 rococo doorway remains from the former church building), and more restoration work was completed in 1996.

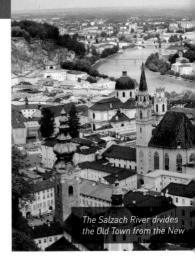
The Salzach River divides the Old Town from the New

Definitely worth a visit is the adjoining **cemetery** (daily summer 9am–6.30pm, winter 9am–4pm), which is surrounded by four arcades, and scattered with tombs, shrines and holy relics. Built by Archbishop Wolf Dietrich, the cemetery is dominated by the **Chapel of St Gabriel** in the centre, which contains his mausoleum. The chapel has a remarkable interior: the walls are clad with tiny coloured ceramic tiles, which contrast dramatically with the brilliant white stucco. The surrounding cemetery is the final resting place of many of Salzburg's best-known names, including Paracelsus, Mozart's widow Constanze and his father Leopold.

MAKARTPLATZ

A short walk northwest from the Staatsbrücke brings you to **Makartplatz**, dominated by the awesome Church of the Holy Trinity (Dreifaltigkeitskirche, 1694–1702). No. 8 Makartplatz is

Mozart's Residence ❷❷ (www.mozarteum.at; daily Sept–June 9am–5.30pm, July–Aug 8.30am–7pm; last entry 30 mins prior to closing; may be closed in Mozart Week in Jan), where the Mozart family lived from 1773 to 1780. The house does not offer much in terms of architectural beauty. It did, however, offer exactly what Leopold Mozart wanted: more space than their former home on the Getreidegasse for the family to live and especially for Wolfgang to work. Indeed, Mozart produced many symphonies, concertos, arias, masses and other sacred music in this house. After he had flown the nest, his mother had died and his sister had married, only Leopold remained in the house.

⊙ THE STIFTUNG MOZARTEUM

In 1880, the International Mozarteum Foundation was formed to 'perform and propagate Mozart's music'. Today, the Foundation runs two museums in the city. Its collections include the composer's original letters and sheet music and numerous performances of his work.

The Foundation is best known for its two long-running concert series. Mozart Week *(Mozartwoche)* is held in late January, with a 10-day presentation of the composer's works to mark his birthday on 27 January. Performances often include concerts by the Vienna Philharmonic Orchestra and concertos by star pianists. In summer, the Foundation's concert series forms a key part of the Salzburg Festival (see page 86).

For Mozart Week information and tickets, contact the Mozarteum Foundation's Ticket Office at Theatergasse 2 (tel: 873 154; www.mozarteum.at). For Salzburg Festival schedules and tickets, visit the festival website at www.salzburger festspiele.at.

After Leopold died in 1787, the house had many owners. It was only in 1989 that the International Mozarteum Foundation was able to purchase the building, which had been rebuilt as an office block after a bomb struck it in 1944. In 1994, the Foundation tore down the office building and began rebuilding according to the original plans of the house. Today it is a museum that displays exhibits from the Mozart family and old musical instruments.

Concert hall in the Mozarteum

Opposite Mozart's family house is the Landestheater (Regional Theatre) and, behind it, the Marionettentheater (Puppet Theatre) and the Stiftung Mozarteum, making this area one of the artistic centres of the city. Built in 1892, the **Landestheater** is the centre of Salzburg's cultural programme, giving performances of all kinds throughout the year, including ballet and opera.

Performances in the **Marionettentheater** (Puppet Theatre) often include full operas enacted by the diminutive wooden characters on strings. The theatre's puppeteers have travelled the world performing their classic operas and plays.

The **Stiftung Mozarteum** ㉓ (Schwarzstrasse 26; www.mozarteum.at) is the headquarters of the foundation of the same name (see box opposite), dedicated to the research and development of Mozart's music. The complex includes concert halls and recital rooms. This institution is not to be confused with the

⊙ SALZBURG AND THE SOUND OF MUSIC

Film lovers will recognise Salzburg and its environs as the setting for *The Sound of Music*. Most people know that the film was based on fact.

The central character, Maria, was born in 1905. A strict upbringing developed an antipathy towards religion in her. After a chance meeting with a priest, she changed her views and joined the Nonnberg Convent. To aid her recovery from an illness, she was sent as governess to the home of Georg von Trapp, a widower with seven children. Love blossomed, Maria and the captain were married and had three children of their own. The von Trapp children were a musical bunch before Maria arrived, but she developed their skills further. When the Austrian Bank closed and Georg was penniless, the children began to sing for money. The von Trapps fled Austria in 1938.

Fans of the movie come here to retrace the big-screen von Trapp family's footsteps. The song *Do Re Mi* was sung in the Mirabell Gardens around the fountain. St Peter's Cemetery was reconstructed in the studios and used for the scene where the von Trapp family hide between tombstones while trying to escape the Nazis. The façade of Frohnburg Castle became the front of the von Trapp villa, while Leopoldskron Castle was the rear. (The real von Trapp villa, at Traunstrasse 34, has been open to guests at the Villa Trapp hotel since 2008, see page 142. Exhibitions were held here in 2015 for the 50th anniversary of the musical.) The opening scenes in the convent were filmed at Nonnberg Convent, the opening credit scenes around Lake Fuschl and the wedding at the church in Mondsee. The von Trapp family make their escape over the Untersberg, in reality this would have taken them straight to Hitler's Eagle's Nest (see page 70).

Universität Mozarteum (east of Mirabell Gardens), the world-famous academy for music and drama (with a wide range of performances).

MIRABELL PALACE AND GARDENS

Next to the Landestheater is the entrance to the **Mirabell-Garten** (Mirabell Gardens) , comprising geometrically designed flowerbeds, fountains, an orangery, a rose garden and lawns adorned with sculptures based on classical mythology. In *The Sound of Music*, this was where Maria and the children danced around the statue of Pegasus singing *Do Re Mi*. On the west side of the parterre is an open-air theatre, with trimmed hedges marking the wings and entrances, and next to it an idyllic shady garden decorated with marble dwarfs (there is also a pleasant children's playground).

In the manicured grounds of Mirabell Palace

The **Mirabell Palace** was built in 1606 by Archbishop Wolf Dietrich, who wanted a residence outside the town walls for his mistress Salome Alt and their children (of whom 10 survived infancy). The archbishop named the palace Altenau. After his imprisonment in the fortress and his death, his nephew and successor Markus Sittikus renamed the palace Mirabell in an attempt to conceal the blasphemous memory of its original purpose. Between 1721 and 1727, the palace was remodelled by Archbishop Franz Anton von Harrach. The stunning marble

Mirabell Palace in the New Town

staircase is the work of Johann Lukas von Hildebrandt, with acrobatic cherubs added by the sculptor Georg Raphael Donner in 1726. The richly adorned **marble hall**, where the Mozart family once performed, was at one time the dining room. Today it is used for concerts and is hugely popular as a wedding venue.

In 1818, the Mirabell was badly damaged in the great fire that ravaged the New Town. Fortunately the marble staircase and hall survived. The current neoclassical style of the palace is thanks to Peter de Nobile, who was the court architect in Vienna and added the detailed work around the windows and the stuccowork.

Many well-known personalities have stayed at the palace, including Prince Otto of Bavaria, who later became the King of Greece, and the legendary Capuchin monk Joachim Haspinger, who died in the palace in 1858. Today, the palace is the office of the Mayor of Salzburg *(Bürgermeister)* and the administration. That is why only certain parts of the building are open to the public (staircase daily 8am–6pm; marble hall Mon, Wed and Thu 8am–4pm, Tue and Fri 1–4pm).

KAPUZINERBERG

Opposite the Hotel Gablerbräu on the Linzergasse is the entrance to the path that leads to the top of **Kapuzinerberg**, Salzburg's highest point at 636m (2,087ft). The hill was inhabited during Neolithic times, and the two settlements above the monastery have been dated to 1000 BC.

On the walk up you pass the six baroque **Stations of the Cross**, which were built between 1736 and 1744. Halfway up is the **Felix Gate**, dating from 1632, which offers the first panoramic view of the city. At this point there is another path called Imbergstiege, which takes you past St John's Chapel and meets up with another path at the *Kanzel* or pulpit, where you will be rewarded by the breathtaking views of the city. Not surprisingly, the forests and quiet location of the Kapuzinerberg make it a haven for wildlife, including deer and badgers.

One cannot climb the Kapuzinerberg without visiting the **Kapuzinerkirche** (Capuchin Monastery) **25**, which was originally a military tower and fortification system erected by nervous archbishops during the Middle Ages. It was Archbishop Wolf Dietrich who called the Capuchin monks to Salzburg in 1594 and

Stefan Zweig

An influential Austrian author, Stefan Zweig (1881–1942) lived in Salzburg between the two world wars. Much translated in the 1930s, Zweig's writings included short stories, novels, literary essays and biographies of Marie Antoinette and Maria Stuart notable for their use of psychoanalytical theories. Although of Jewish origin, he described himself as an 'accidental Jew'.

transformed the fortification into a monastery and church. The monastery is surrounded by a wall, which runs from the Felix Gate and straddles the western, southern and eastern slopes. The towering cross and bastion of the monastery are dominant features of the landscape, though the monastery itself is very modest. The Gothic oak door of the inner portal is said to be a relic from the old Salzburg Cathedral. The interior of the monastery church is simple, befitting a life of devotion.

Kapuzinerberg 5 is the former residence of the writer Stefan Zweig, who chose the house for its tranquil location. Having lived in Salzburg since 1919, he fled Austria in 1934 following Hitler's rise to power. He first lived in England (in Bath and London) and then the US before moving to Brazil in 1941, where he and his wife both committed suicide because of their concern for the future of Europe. There is a memorial to Zweig next to the Capuchin Monastery.

SALZBURG'S ENVIRONS

LEOPOLDSKRON LAKE AND PALACE

A short walk south from the Nonntal area of the Old Town takes you to the Leopoldskron district, which contains the lake and palace of the same name. The **Schloss Leopoldskron** (Leopoldskron Palace) ㉖ was built by Archbishop Firmian in 1736 in rococo style. The archbishops used the palace for centuries, but in the early 20th century, it was bought by Max Reinhardt, one of the founders of the Salzburg Festival. He had it totally renovated and the gardens laid out in their present form. Now the property of an American institute, it is used for conferences and seminars but unfortunately is not open to the public. However, you can see the palace from the lakeside path, which provides a lovely walk at any

Inside the spectacular glass dome at Hangar-7

time of year. In the summer, the swans are wonderful to watch and in winter, the Salzburgers love to use the lake for ice-skating and curling matches.

The lake and the house featured in the filming of *The Sound of Music*. The rear of the house was used as the von Trapp villa and the boating scene was filmed on the lake.

HANGAR-7

If you are in the vicinity of the airport, it's worth paying a visit to **Hangar-7** ㉗ (Wilhelm-Spazier-Strasse 7A; www.hangar-7. com; daily 9am–10pm; free). Completed in 2003, it was built to house a collection of vintage aircraft. The hangar is a glass and steel dome in the shape of an aircraft wing and constitutes one of the highlights of modern architecture in Salzburg. Situated on the eastern apron of Salzburg's airport, there are two buildings. The first and largest is the hangar that is open to the public. Facing and mirroring it on a smaller scale is Hangar-8, the maintenance hangar.

The museum on the ground floor not only houses aircraft, but also Formula 1 racing cars from the Red Bull teams. During the summer months, many of the aircraft are at various air shows around Europe and may not all be on display. However, there are changing art exhibitions to view throughout the year. There is also a bar, a café and a top-class restaurant, Ikarus (see page 112).

STIEGL'S BRAUWELT

Not far from the airport and Hangar-7 is **Stiegl's Brauwelt** ㉘ (Stiegl's World of Brewing; Bräuhausstrasse 9; www.stiegl.at; daily July–Aug 10am–7pm, Sept–June 10am–5pm; last entry 1 hour prior to closing). Stiegl, probably the favourite local brew in Salzburg, is served in many of the pubs and restaurants around town. The brewery has been here for over 500 years and is the oldest one that is privately owned in Austria.

Attached to the brewery is a museum housing the world's largest beer exhibition. There is a display of brewing techniques, machinery and unusual equipment through the ages. The tour reveals how the beer is produced and provides a chance to taste some samples.

HELLBRUNN PALACE

A short bus ride (route No. 25) from the railway station takes you south to **Hellbrunn Palace and Gardens** ㉙ (Schloss Hellbrunn; www.hellbrunn.at; palace open daily Apr and Oct 9am–4.30pm, May–June and Sept 9am–5.30pm, July–Aug 9am–9pm; gardens open daily summer 6am–9pm, winter 6.30am–5pm; park and orangery free). The palace was built between 1613 and 1615 as a hunting lodge and summer residence for Markus Sittikus. Its architect, Santino Solari, was also the man responsible for the

The 17th-century Hellbrunn Palace

reconstruction of Salzburg Cathedral. The Hellbrunn Festival is held in the palace and gardens every August.

The palace itself is not very large, and the interior is no longer complete, but it's worth visiting to see the wonderful Italian murals in the banqueting hall and the adjoining music room in the octagonal pavilion. The palace's **trick fountains** also delight visitors. Markus Sittikus had these built to amuse himself and his guests (but particularly himself). The **Roman Theatre** has stone seats that spew out water without warning, so Sittikus' guests would be unexpectedly soaked (as visitors still are today). Funnily enough, this does not happen to the archbishop's chair at the top. There are also many charming grottoes featuring similar watery surprises based on mythological themes. If you are carrying expensive camera equipment, make sure you are ready to cover it up quickly. Hydraulics also drive a large **mechanical theatre**, with moving figures and an organ that runs on water power.

Trick fountain at Hellbrunn Palace

The park area surrounding the palace dates from 1730, although some of its sculptures are from the early 17th century and include a statue of Empress Elisabeth. The pavilion that was used in *The Sound of Music* was relocated here from its original place at Leopoldskron.

Also in the grounds, about a 20-minute walk from the palace, is the Stone Theatre, formed by a natural gorge, where the first opera in the German-speaking world was presented in 1617.

On Hellbrunn Mountain, still inside the park, stands the Monatsschlössl (Month Castle), so-called because it was allegedly built in only one month. It houses a **Folklore Museum** (Volkskunde Museum; www.salzburgmuseum.at; daily Apr–Oct 10am–5.30pm), which displays costumes, masks, religious artefacts and agricultural equipment from the lively history of Salzburg.

Also on the mountain is **Salzburg Zoo** (www.salzburg-zoo.at; daily Nov–Feb 9am–4.30pm, Mar until 5.30pm, Apr–May and Sept–Oct until 6pm, June–Aug until 6.30pm; last entry Apr–Oct 1 hour prior to closing). There has been a zoo on this site since 1421. Originally, it housed only alpine animals, but it has since been extended to include species from all over the world. Over 800 creatures can be seen here – many of them (no dangerous ones) allowed to roam freely around the grounds and beyond. There are often monkeys on the paths, storks in the nearby fields and vultures circling in the thermals above the Untersberg. From August until early September, the zoo is open on Friday and Saturday evenings until 10.30pm (last entry 9pm) for 'Night Zoo' sessions, when the nocturnal animals are the star performers.

KLESSHEIM PALACE

The main part of **Schloss Klessheim** (Klessheim Palace) ㉚, about 1.5km (1 mile) west of the city centre (No. 18 bus), was built by Austria's greatest baroque architect, Johann Fischer von Erlach, for Archbishop Johann Ernst Graf Thun between 1700 and 1709. He used designs and ideas from Versailles palace and gardens and eventually completed the construction in 1732.

⊘ THE FÖHN

Situated so close to the Alps, Salzburg experiences a phenomenon called the *Föhn* for about 45 days of the year. A *Föhn* is created when air is forced up one side of a mountain range, causing it to expand and cool and lose its water vapour. When the dry air starts to move down the north side of the Alps, it warms as the pressure increases, creating strong, gusty, warm and dry winds. When a *Föhn* blows into Salzburg, it is enough to lay the whole city low. Headaches, asthma attacks and frayed nerves are common; the suicide rate, crime and traffic accidents increase. However, a *Föhn* day is generally a lovely day, bringing subtropical temperatures in summer and warm, pleasant days in winter.

It was used by the archbishops until Salzburg came under the control of the Habsburgs. In the late 19th century, Emperor Franz Josef banished his homosexual younger brother, Archduke Ludwig Viktor, to Klessheim Palace after Ludwig had sparked a public scandal by making advances to an army officer in a swimming pool in Vienna. He died here in 1919.

Between 1938 and 1945, Hitler used the palace as his residence when he was in Salzburg. It was here that he met the Italian dictator Mussolini in 1940 and other heads of state from Hungary, Czechoslovakia and Romania. After the war, it became the headquarters of the occupying army. Then for a long time it was used by the provincial government to receive important state visitors such as Queen Elizabeth II.

Since 1993, it has housed the only year-round **casino** in Salzburg Province. You can enjoy the gardens and a few rooms of the palace free, but to enter the casino (daily 3pm–3am) there is an admission fee which provides you with your first gaming chips. Minimum age for entry is 18 and you must provide some photo identification. As well as the No. 1 bus from the city centre, shuttle buses operated by the casino run from 5.30pm from town to the casino (tel: 854 455), returning hourly from 5pm to any location in town.

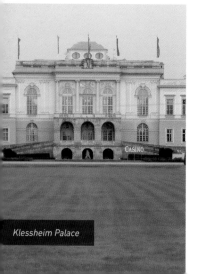

Klessheim Palace

View of the Untersberg from the Mönchsberg

SOUTH OF SALZBURG

UNTERSBERG

The highest mountain in the vicinity of Salzburg is the **Untersberg** 🛐 , to the southwest. It can be seen for kilometres around as it juts up from the flatlands and towers 1,853m (6,078ft) above sea level. The mountain is a limestone massif with deposits of salt and marble. The terrain is craggy and steep, making it a strenuous climb on foot. If you do not have a car, you can take bus No. 25 to the bottom station of the cable car in **Grödig** (daily July–Sept 8.30am–5.30pm, Mar–June and Oct–Nov 8.30am–5pm, Jan–Feb and Dec 9am–4pm). Alternatively, there is a cycle path that takes you all the way there. On a clear day, the views from the top are incredible. You can see the whole of the Salzburg basin, into Bavaria, the Watzmann (the second highest mountain in Germany) and as far as the Lake District (Salzkammergut) to the east and the Hohe Tauern mountains in the south. There are a few easy walks from the top station of the cable car to the viewpoints. For those who do not want to venture too far, there is a panoramic view from the top station.

⊘ LEGENDS OF THE UNTERSBERG

According to legend, dwarfs, giants and wild virgins all live on the Untersberg. However, the mountain's main mythical character is Emperor Karl the Great, who is said to sleep within the mountain. Legend foretells a time when the ravens that circle the summit will stop and the Emperor's beard will have grown three times around a marble table. Then he will rise and fight the battle of good versus evil. The venue for this battle is quite specific: the pear tree in Wals. Once victorious, the Emperor will hang up his shield and an era of happiness and prosperity will follow. Other legends view the rising of the Emperor as Judgement Day, when the Antichrist will appear and do battle with angels.

Less portentously, historians debate the importance of the Untersberg during Celtic times, when Salzburg was geographically almost central in the Celtic empire. Given the pattern of early settlements found around Salzburg, it may be that the Untersberg was of great religious importance, and many of the mountain's legends have possible links with the political and religious propaganda of the early Middle Ages. Certainly few mountains in the Alps have generated such colourful mythology.

Countryside surrounding Berchtesgaden

Tucked beneath the northwest slopes of the Untersberg is the village of **Grossgmain** ㉜, which has an **Open-Air Museum** (Freilichtmuseum; www.freilichtmuseum.com; July–Aug daily 9am–6pm, late-Mar–June, Sept–early Oct Tue–Sun 9am–6pm, early Oct–early Nov 9am–5pm, late Dec–early Jan 9am–4pm; last entry 1 hour before closing). The museum is one of the top attractions in the area and has won numerous awards. It includes a collection of around 100 old farmhouses that have been transferred from different parts of Salzburg Province and reconstructed with meticulous care. They span the last five centuries, showing how building and farming methods have changed and developed.

There are also many old farm machines to be viewed, and on Sundays and public holidays craftsmen demonstrate the old trades, from woodwork to beekeeping, shoemaking to beer-brewing. The museum covers an area of 50 hectares (125 acres), so you will need a full day to see it all.

BERCHTESGADEN

Just 30km (18 miles) south of Salzburg, across the border in Germany, is **Berchtesgaden** ㉝. Set amid beautiful alpine scenery dominated by the impressive peaks of Germany's second-highest mountain, the Watzmann (2,713m/8,900ft), this delightful little town encapsulates all the attractions of the Bavarian Alps, including painted houses and wonderful views. But the area also has a dark side. The village of **Obersalzberg**, just above the town, was where in 1934 Hitler bought a chalet known as the Berghof (Mountain House), and had it decorated in the most pretentious style, with massive furniture and heavy fireplaces. It became his country retreat, where he entertained his cronies, Nazi Party functionaries and, in 1938, Neville Chamberlain, the British prime minister. A Gestapo headquarters was established nearby, and beneath it all was a network of underground bunkers. Most of these buildings, including the Berghof, were destroyed in an Allied air raid in 1945, and the remains were blown up by the West German government in 1953.

In the village, the fascinating **Dokumentation Obersalzberg** (www.obersalzberg.de; Apr–Oct daily 9am–5pm, Nov–Mar Tue–Sun 10am–3pm; last entry 1 hour prior to closing) explains the bigger picture of the Third Reich.

You can still visit the Kehlsteinhaus or Eagle's Nest – the 'teahouse' built by Martin Bormann as Hitler's 50th birthday present from the Nazi Party (www.kehlsteinhaus.de; daily mid-May–mid-Oct). It sits precariously on the top of Kehlstein mountain at 1,834m (6,017ft). Parking for cars is in Obersalzberg, where you can catch a bus to the summit, up a mountain road that was built specifically to reach the Eagle's Nest, a remarkable feat of engineering. Once at the top, you board the original brass-lined lift for the 124m (406ft) ascent to the house itself. Part of it is now a restaurant and provides fantastic views.

Also located in the Berchtesgaden area are the ancient **Salt Mines** (Salzbergwerk; www.salzbergwerk.de; tours daily May–Oct 9am–5pm, Nov–Mar 11am–3pm, Apr 10am–3pm). Salt has been mined here since 1517, and still is today. Visitors are issued with old miners' clothing to take a tour of the mines, accompanied by a miner (you also get an audio guide), starting in a small wagon on railway tracks. The rest of the tour includes sliding down a miners' chute and taking a ferry across an underground salt lake. One feature not to be missed is the 'chapel', a grotto of oddly shaped salt formations illuminated to eerie effect.

KÖNIGSSEE

To the south of Berchtesgaden, and within the Alpen Nationalpark Berchtesgaden, lies **Königssee** ③④, one of the most beautiful

A tranquil scene at Königssee with St Bartholomä

SALZBERGBAU
DÜRRNBERG

Dürrnberg Salt Mines

lakes in the region. The narrow fjord-like lake runs 9km (5.6 miles) north–south in the shadow of the Watzmann, its giant east face rising almost straight out of the water. There is a car park near the small village of Königssee, at the northern end of the 192m (630ft) deep 'fjord'. From here you can take a boat trip along the whole length of the lake. As only a small part of Königssee is visible from the village, the trip is highly recommended, to fully appreciate the stunning beauty of the scenery. The first stop (and final one in winter) is **St Bartholomä**, where there is a pretty baroque church with twin onion domes and a restaurant serving wonderfully fresh fish from the lake. The second is **Salet** at the lake's southern tip. There is a commentary on board in English about the lake's history, and the aims of the Alpine National Park Berchtesgaden and the Unesco Biosphere Reserve. To keep pollution levels down the tourist boats are electric and, apart from rescue boats and farmers' boats, they are the only powered craft allowed on the lake.

HALLEIN

About 15km (10 miles) south of Salzburg lies the busy little town of **Hallein** ㉟, the second-largest town in Salzburg Province and the district capital of the Tennengau. You can reach it either by train or by car via the A10 Tauern motorway.

Hallein has a delightful old town on the banks of the Salzach River. Most of the houses in the old town were built in the late Middle Ages, and many were renovated in the 1980s. Until the early 1990s, the town's Perner Island was an industrial site with a large salt processing plant, but it has now been turned into a cultural centre and every year stages a number of performances during the Salzburg Festival.

A large paper mill is the town's main employer, but in former years salt mining brought wealth to Hallein. Salt was discovered on the Dürrnberg by the Celts, and was mined there as recently as 1989. Now the mines are closed and have been turned into a museum. A tour of the **Dürrnberg Salt Mines** (Salzwelten; www.salzwelten.at; guided tours daily, Apr–Oct 9am–5pm, Nov–Mar 10am–3pm) demonstrates how salt was mined, explains the importance of salt and gives visitors the chance to go on an underground boat trip and to slide down an old miners' chute. Also included in the Salzwelten ticket is the **Celtic Village**, a reconstruction of a village showing how the Celts lived and worked.

Back in the town, the **Celtic Museum** (Pflegerplatz 5; www.salzburgmuseum.at; daily 9am–5pm) houses a fascinating collection of archaeological finds from the area, including equipment used

Franz Xaver Gruber's grave

Hohenwerfen Castle

by the miners, as well as priceless burial offerings. The **Silent Night Museum** (Gruberplatz 1; www.salzburgmuseum. at; closed for restoration until September 2018) is a celebration of the famous Christmas carol whose composer, Franz Xaver Gruber (1787–1863), is buried in Hallein in front of his house (museum). He was organist and choirmaster here since 1835, but composed the famous carol as early as 1818, when teaching at a primary school in the village of Arnsdorf.

WERFEN

If you continue south from Hallein along the A10 for another 29km (18 miles), you reach **Werfen** 36, a small market town situated on what was an important trade route for salt. The town is strung along a wide road and is pleasant to walk through. The parish church, built between 1652 and 1657, contains a very impressive baroque altar and early baroque side altars.

Castle Hohenwerfen (www.salzburg-burgen.at/en/hohen werfen-castle; Apr and Oct–mid-Nov Tue–Sun 9.30am–4pm, May–mid-July and mid-Aug–Sept daily 9am–5pm, mid-July–mid-Aug daily 9am–6pm) was built in 1077 to guard the trade route. Frequent additions up to the 16th century have given it a fairy-tale appearance. It was used as a prison for many centuries and among those locked up there was Archbishop Wolf Dietrich von Raitenau in 1611. According to folklore, the dungeons in these castles were sometimes filled to capacity with innocent people, including Protestant missionaries who had offended the archbishops of Salzburg in some way. It is said that these 'unwanted sorts' were locked up in darkness in solitary confinement for years and only set free after they had gone mad.

The castle has an interesting armoury and Austria's first **falconry museum**, and there are falconry displays several times a day. The castle was used as a location for the 1968 film *Where Eagles Dare*.

EISRIESENWELT

The caves of **Eisriesenwelt** (World of the Ice Giants; www.eisriesenwelt.at; guided tours daily May–June and Sept–Oct 8am–3pm; July–Aug until 4pm; charge includes cable car), northeast of Werfen, are the largest ice caves in Europe. They stretch for about 42km (26 miles), although only a fraction of that length is open to the public. Fantastic ice 'statues' and frozen waterfalls extend for about 1km (0.5 mile) from the entrance. The ice formations are created during the winter months when the water in the caves freezes, so the best time to see them is in the spring and early summer before the formations have started to melt again.

Drive or take a bus from Werfen's main square, to the car park by the visitor centre. Then it's a 20-minute walk to the cable-car station. In order to enter the caves, you have to take one of the many guided tours that start at regular intervals. As the temperature inside is always around freezing point, wear warm clothing – and sensible shoes to negotiate the narrow slippery passages. The caves are not recommended for the elderly, infirm or young children. Although it's quite a strenuous excursion, it is certainly worth the effort.

THE GROSSGLOCKNER ROAD

One of the most spectacular scenic routes through the Alps is the **Grossglockner High Alpine Road** ㊲ (Grossglockner Hochalpenstrasse). The Grossglockner itself is Austria's highest mountain at 3,798m (12,460ft). It is situated in the Hohe Tauern range of mountains and in the national park of the same name, which straddles the provinces of Salzburg, East Tyrol and Carinthia.

The job of planning the road, running 48km (30 miles) between Bruck and Heiligenblut, was given to the engineer Franz Wallack in 1924. Construction started in 1930, taking five years. The road had to be rebuilt after World War II, having been seriously damaged by tank movements. Until the Felbertauern tunnel was built, this was the main road linking the provinces

Rural encounter

of Salzburg and Carinthia via the Alps. Since 1935, some 60 million people have made use of the road. It is popular with cyclists, motorcyclists – there are special facilities for parking motorbikes and equipment lockers along the route – car drivers and coach groups. On some sunny summer days, there can be thousands of people making the pilgrimage along this road.

A toll road, it is officially open from the beginning of May until early November (www.grossglockner.at; daily May 6am–8pm, June–Aug 5am–9.30pm, Sept–late Oct 6am–7.30pm, late Oct–early Nov 8am–5pm, last entry 45 mins before closing), but sometimes summer snowfalls can close it for days at a time. Before you set off, it's worth checking with the Ferleiten Information Point (tel: 6546 650) whether the road is actually open or not. The ticket you buy at the tollbooth gives you access to the road's exhibitions and sights.

There are various **viewpoints** to stop at along the way. The Fuscher Törl, which lies at 2,428m (7,966ft) above sea level, has a memorial built by Clemens Holzmeister to commemorate those who died during the construction of the road. The highest point of the through road is the Hochtor at 2,503m (8,212ft). You will be quite likely to find snow up here even in August. But if you take the detour to the Franz-Josefs-Höhe, which is highly recommended, you can reach an even higher point called the Edelweissspitze, at 2,571m (8,435ft).

You have the best view of the Grossglockner from the Franz-Josefs-Höhe (2,369m/7,772ft), where there is a lift that takes you down to the Pasterze Glacier (note that the glacier is shrinking and so the bottom of the lift is now about 300m/yds away from the start of the glacier). This is where you are most likely to see marmots lying in the sun – or hear their whistles when alarmed. Access to walks and visitor centres are included in your ticket.

The road takes you through a variety of vegetation zones and is quite fascinating. There are also many activities to do with the family at places such as Fuscher Lake, at 2,262m (7,421ft), where there is an exhibition about the construction of the road. There is a geology path and, at Schöneck, a botanical path. Various restaurants are dotted along the route, but it is recommended to avoid lunchtimes at the

Franz-Josefs-Höhe, as the restaurants there are very busy catering for the numerous coach parties.

KRIMML WATERFALLS

At the very western end of the Salzach Valley, just before the **Gerlos road** starts its steep ascent over the pass to the Tyrol, lie the **Krimml Waterfalls** ❸ (Krimmler Wasserfälle; daily mid-Apr–Oct; free in winter, but there is no guarantee that the path will be passable and safe). Like the Grossglockner, they are part of the Hohe Tauern National Park. With a drop of 380m (1,247ft), the Krimmler Wasserfälle are the highest waterfalls in Europe and make a magnificent spectacle as they plunge down the mountainside in three stages. The falls are at their most impressive in the spring and early summer when

Krimml Waterfalls in the Hohe Tauern National Park

the melt-waters turn the stream into a torrent. The Krimmler Ache starts at the Krimmler Kees glacier before plummeting down the falls.

The path up to the falls is relatively steep, but not difficult, and there are benches and viewing platforms all along the route where you can rest your legs while admiring the rainbow colours in the spray of the falls.

The first waterfall is 140m (460ft) high and the most spectacular of the three. This one can be viewed from the bottom without any strenuous walking. The walk from the car park will take around 10 minutes. Walking from the bottom of the first falls to the second, which is 100m (330ft) high, will take half an hour. Then to the top falls (a 140m/460ft drop), it's another hour's climb. Allow plenty of time to get back before nightfall.

The falls have been popular with visitors for many years. The first rough steps to the top of the first falls were built in 1835. The existing path was completed in 1897, built by the local branch of the Alpine Club. For keen walkers there are several further trails that can be explored from the top of the falls.

In *WasserWunderWelt* (The Wonderful World of Water) at the bottom of the falls, information panels describe the flora and fauna in the area, as well as hydro-energy. There is also a multivision cinema.

THE SALZKAMMERGUT

The Salzkammergut (Salt Chamber Estate) refers to the wealth that salt brought to the region, but it is an area that today is more famous for its lakes and alpine scenery than for its salt industry, and is also known as the Lake District. The area

On the shore of Fuschlsee

extends from Fuschl near Salzburg to the Almtal in the east, with impressive peaks and more than 70 lakes. It is one of Austria's most popular tourist regions and often considered to be the jewel of the nation. The area has been popular with visitors since Emperor Franz Josef spent his summers in Bad Ischl.

FUSCHLSEE

The first lake you come to heading east from Salzburg is **Fuschlsee** ❸❾. About 25km (15 miles) from the city, it can be reached by the A1 motorway or along the B1/B158 (the prettier route). The lake is 4km (2.5 miles) long and wonderfully warm in the summer. The steep, wooded slopes rising along its shore curve to its eastern shore where the village of Fuschl lies. This quiet little resort is popular with walkers in the summer and also offers water sports. If the countryside looks familiar, it may be that you recognise it from the opening titles of *The Sound of Music*, which was filmed here.

On the opposite shore, in its own extensive grounds, is Schloss Fuschl. This was originally a hunting lodge of the prince archbishops, then during World War II it was used as headquarters by Hitler's Foreign Minister Joachim von Ribbentrop. Since the late 1950s it has been a luxury hotel, with its own golf course, where Richard Nixon and Nikita Krushchev, among other notables, have been entertained.

WOLFGANGSEE

About 7km (4.5 miles) further southeast from Fuschl lies the quaint little village of St Gilgen. Stretched along the northern shore of **Wolfgangsee** ⑩ (Wolfgang Lake), it is a popular destination for holidaymakers in summer and winter. The Wolfgangsee itself is 10km (6 miles) long and 2km (1.2 miles) wide. With water temperatures of around 26°C (78°F) in summer, it is popular for a variety of water sports.

St Gilgen is famed as the birthplace of Mozart's mother, Anna Pertl (1720–78). Although the composer himself never came here, there is now a **Mozart** multimedia show (June–Sept Tue–Sun 10am–noon and 3–6pm) in the house where his mother was born. His sister Nannerl also lived in the house after her marriage, but she moved to Salzburg in 1801 when

Picturesque façades in the village of St Gilgen

her husband died. The Mozart fountain and the parish church (1376) are also worth a visit.

For walkers and skiers, the Zwölferhorn lift takes you to the top of the **Zwölferhorn** mountain at 1,522m (4,993ft). In summer, the summit is a starting point for many alpine walks, while in winter, beginners and families ski here.

The village is also a good place from which to take a boat across the lake to **St Wolfgang**. The boats – some of which date from the 1880s – run a regular service from April to October. The journey is a wonderful way to appreciate the beauty of the countryside. Alternatively, you can drive the 18km (11 miles) along the whole of the southern shore of the lake and along most of the northern shore until you reach St Wolfgang.

This village is probably the most overtly touristy of all the locations on the Wolfgangsee, but when you see it hugging the shore and protected by the Schafberg towering 1,783m (5,850ft) above it, you will understand why. The village has a long history as a pilgrimage destination following its foundation in 976 by St Wolfgang, the bishop of Regensburg. According to legend, he built the village's first small church, which is allegedly a site of miracle cures. It is certainly one of the most beautiful churches in the region. Inside, it has a winged altar created by Michael Pacher in 1481 and three baroque altars by Meinrad Guggenbichler from 1706.

The village is also famous for its White Horse Inn, a hotel with a wonderful lakeside terrace. It was the inspiration for Ralph Benatzky's operetta *Im Weissen Rössl am Wolfgangsee*, which was first performed in Berlin in 1930.

A trip up the **Schafberg** on the funicular railway (mid-May–late Oct) is not to be missed. On a clear day, you have the most breathtaking view of the Salzkammergut with its lakes and mountains spread below. The railway was built at the end of the 19th century and has been operational for over 100 years. For steam train enthusiasts, the old steam-fired train does occasional nostalgia trips. For timetable and fare information, see www.schafbergbahn.at.

Sailing on the Wolfgangsee

MONDSEE

The nearby lake of **Mondsee** lies approximately 30km (19m) east of Salzburg and is easily reached on the A1 motorway. An alternative route is the Romantikstrasse from St Gilgen, taking you under the Schafberg and along the western shore of the Mondsee. The lake has a reputation for being the warmest in the Salzkammergut and it is popular for all kinds of water sports in summer. The market town of Mondsee is worth visiting to see its church, originally part of a large Benedictine monastery. It was founded in 748, although construction of the church began in 1470. Built in Gothic style, it has a 17th-century baroque interior. This was where the wedding scene in *The Sound of Music* was filmed.

The extensive Neolithic stilt settlements in the lake, which are well documented in the **Pfahlbaumuseum** (www.pfahl bauten.de; Apr–Sept daily 9am–7pm, Oct–Mar schedules vary, so check the website) were given Unesco World Heritage status in 2011.

Salzburg province is ideal for mountain bikers, from novice to experienced

WHAT TO DO

Salzburg is a very agreeable city for sightseeing. Most of the major sights are within easy walking distance of the centre. You can stroll around the Old Town, wander into the cathedral and other churches, relax in the large spacious squares, play outdoor chess, take a *Fiaker* (horse-drawn carriage) ride around the city or climb up the hill to see the fortress.

A pleasant way to relax in high summer is to sit on the grassy riverbank and watch the fast-flowing waters of the Salzach flow by, as well as the hustle and bustle of city life. If you want to get on the water, you can take a boat trip on the *Amadeus Salzburg*, which docks near the Makartsteg (pedestrian bridge). This takes you up the river as far as Hellbrunn and back again (www.salzburghighlights.at).

CULTURE AND NIGHTLIFE

It is impossible to ignore Mozart in Salzburg. There is his birthplace, the house that he grew up in, Mozartplatz with its statue of Mozart, Mozartsteg (bridge), the Mozart Festival, *Mozartkugeln* (mini chocolate balls filled with marzipan) and the Wolfgang Amadeus Mozart Airport. But young Wolfgang is far from the only cultural feature of this city. The museums and galleries offer

Mozart's 250th

In 2006, Salzburg played a major role in the 250th birthday celebrations of Mozart. The festivities included a rare staging of all 22 of Mozart's operas during the Salzburg Festival.

everything from Stone Age relics and Roman remains to vintage aeroplanes and modern art.

Music and the performing arts are everywhere. All year round, operas and concerts are performed in the Festival Halls. The Landestheater (state theatre) and smaller theatres host musicals, ballets, operas and drama.

FESTIVALS

The internationally famous **Salzburg Festival** (Salzburger Festspiele) is held every year from mid-July to the end of August. Throughout the day you can hear opera singers practising

⊘ WINTER WONDERLAND

From the beginning of December until 6 January (Epiphany), the city becomes a winter wonderland, taken over by Christmas market stalls, ice sculptures, food and *Glühwein* stands and carol singers. It is a great social occasion enjoyed by residents and tourists alike. The largest Christmas market is held on Residenzplatz and Domplatz, while Mozartplatz becomes an ice rink. There are other markets in Mirabell Platz, Sterngarten (near the Sternbräu restaurant just off Getreidegasse), the Fortress Courtyard (weekends only) and Hellbrunn Palace.

On 6 December, St Nikolaus Day, the saint delivers his bag of goodies (traditionally chocolate) to well-behaved children. However, on 5 December, the city is visited by the Krampus – a devil-like horned creature who rushes around punishing naughty children. In fact, there are usually several Krampuses at large; you will know they are near when you hear their bells or the screams of the children. Keep a safe distance: Krampuses have permission to hit people!

through open windows, and every evening the Festival Halls and squares play host to magnificent operas and orchestral concerts. During the six-week period almost 200 events take place, including operas, concerts, plays and ballets, attracting the highest calibre of artists. If you are visiting Salzburg at this time and have not booked well in advance, there is very little accommodation to be had.

Open-air performance during the Salzburg Festival

Many other festivals take place in Salzburg throughout the year. Among them is **Mozartwoche**, held each January (see page 95). The **Easter Festival**, every March or early April, sees the Staatskapelle Dresden relocate to Salzburg for two weeks to perform various operatic and orchestral productions. The **Pfingstfestspiele** (Whitsun Festival), a four-day festival of baroque music, takes place in May over the Whitsun weekend.

Karneval (Carnival) is the ball season all over Austria, and in the Roman Catholic areas of Germany. The ball season begins properly with the New Year's Eve celebrations and continues right up to Shrove Tuesday *(Faschingsdienstag)*, the last day before Lent (normally in February), when it culminates in a big celebration in which everybody dresses up in fancy dress and goes out to party. New Year's Eve and *Fasching* are the only two days of the year when the bars and taverns do not have to close.

All through the summer many individual streets hold festivals as well, with stalls and street theatre. In late August or early September, the **harvest festivals** begin, running until Austria's National Day on 26 October. Numerous events take place in the city of Salzburg and all the towns and villages in the province. These include church thanksgiving services, brass band music (with sausages and beer), craft and farmers' markets, carved pumpkin displays, petting farms and other activities for children, and the taking down of the maypole that has been standing since the beginning of May. You will recognise the places holding harvest festivals by the large hay statues creatively constructed from bales and other paraphernalia. Take the opportunity to sample the local products, such as *Sturm* (fermented grape juice). Stiegl (the local brewery) normally brings out an autumn beer too.

Salzburg's Christmas market

NIGHTLIFE

Salzburg's varied nightlife offers bars, pubs, wine bars and taverns to suit all ages, tastes and budgets. Taverns like Zum Fidelen Affen and Gasthaus Zum Wilden Mann are a must for beer lovers who want to experience the Austrian brew at its finest. Food is normally served here as well. The main streets for bars are Rudolfskai, Gstättengasse, Kaigasse, Giselakai and Steingasse. Club-like bars, such as Republic and the Shamrock Irish Bar, have designated dance areas and live music.

For fans of Mozart, the **Mozart Dinner Concert** in St Peter Stiftskulinarium (tel: 841 2680; www.stpeter.at/en/mozart-dinner.html) is the perfect evening entertainment. Exquisite soloists and a small chamber orchestra perform pieces of *Don Giovanni*, *The Marriage of Figaro* and *The Magic Flute* between the three courses of a meal prepared according to traditional 18th-century recipes.

Between mid-May and October, you might consider the 'Sound of Salzburg Dinner Show', an entertainment-and-dining package all in English. The show takes place at the Sternbräu Dinner Theater, Griesgasse 23 (tel: 231 05800; www.soundofsalzburg.info), and begins with a video entitled *Maria von Trapp – the True Story*. The stage show includes melodies from *The Sound of Music*, a 'Trapp Family Folk Music Revival' and a tribute to Mozart, performed in period costumes.

SHOPPING

Salzburg has plenty of outlets for the dedicated shopper: modern shopping centres, specialist stores and antique shops, designer boutiques and high-street fashion, and several wonderful markets selling fresh produce, arts, crafts and souvenir trinkets. The shopping centres are just a short bus ride from the

Shopping on Universitätsplatz

centre of town (Europark, route No. 1 or 6, and Alpenstrasse, No. 3, 5 or 8), but everything else is within walking distance.

The main shopping streets in the city centre are **Getreidegasse**, in the Old Town, and **Linzergasse**, across the river in the New Town. Here you will find individual designer boutiques and chain stores alongside bakeries, jewellers and supermarkets. If you explore the many lanes that lead off Getreidegasse to Universitätsplatz, Judengasse, Kaigasse, Papagenoplatz and Steingasse, you will come across shops that deal in antiques, art, sculptures, perfumes, handmade soap, shoes, music and gifts. You can even buy Christmas tree decorations and Easter eggs all year round.

There's a fresh produce market, called **Grünmarkt**, Monday to Saturday on Universitätsplatz, where vegetables, fruit, meat, poultry, fish, seafood, pastries, cheeses, flowers, crafts and spices create a feast of colours and smells. The

Schrannenmarkt is similar, held every Thursday 5am–1pm in front of St Andrew's Church on Mirabellplatz. In both of these markets are many snack stands selling traditional treats, which are worth trying. From the end of May until September there is a market called **Salzachgalerien** held on some weekends on the Old Town riverbank of the Salzach. This is where local artists and craftspeople come to display and sell their work.

SPORTS

The city and the province of Salzburg offer a wide range of activities for all seasons. During the winter you have the option of downhill and cross-country skiing, snowboarding, ice skating and tobogganing. In summer you can choose from golf, hiking, horse riding, summer tobogganing, mountain biking and climbing, paragliding, water sports and canyoning or white-water rafting. Check with the tourist information office, the receptionist in your hotel or in youth hostels for up-to-date information on companies offering activity excursions.

WINTER SPORTS

Salzburg's professional ice hockey team, the Red Bulls, have their home arena in the Volksgarten (Eisarena). The hockey season starts in late August and continues until March. If you are in Salzburg and the team is playing, you should get tickets as early as possible from the Eisarena (tel: 564 311; https://ecrbs.redbulls.com). It is advisable to dress warmly.

From the first snowfall, children make the field behind the fortress their winter playground. Makeshift toboggans compete with high-tech versions in sliding down the hill. Anyone is free to join in, and there is no entrance fee.

Off-piste skiing

Salzburg is a well-located city for skiing and snowboarding, with some of the best slopes in the world within relatively easy reach. The province has hosted the Alpine Skiing World Championships, as well as ski jumping and snowboarding competitions. Whether you are an absolute beginner or an experienced skier, you will find a slope to suit your needs. Most of the major ski resorts are to the south of Salzburg, the nearest being just 20 minutes away and the best of them between 45 and 90 minutes from the city. The resorts offer a wide choice of accommodation, including slope-side alpine cabins, as well as numerous shops, restaurants, banks and a good nightlife. Off-piste skiing, cross-country, ice skating, tobogganing and night skiing are just some of the additional activities. Among the ski areas within comfortable travelling distance of Salzburg are Flachau, Obertauern, Badgastein, Zell Am See and Saalbach-Hinterglemm.

The best way to get to the resorts from Salzburg is by train, leaving early in the morning. The information desk at the railway station will be able to advise you about the best way to reach your destination. If you are staying in Salzburg during the winter season and would like to go skiing for just one or two days, a free Salzburg–Flachau Ski Bus leaves Mirabellplatz every morning at 8.30am to Flachau (return at 4pm). There is also the Kitzbühler Alpen Shuttle from Salzburg Airport.

WATER SPORTS

Salzburg offers a choice of attractive outdoor swimming pools, which are well maintained and very clean. All have lifeguards on duty, as well as snack bars and restaurants. Some even have diving pools and crazy golf. The outdoor pools *(Freibad)* are at the following locations: Leopoldskron (bus No. 22), Volksgarten (bus No. 6 or 7) and Alpenstrasse (bus No. 3 or 8). There is also an indoor swimming pool in the city centre at Paracelsus Bad & Kurhaus, Auerspergstrasse 2. If you would prefer to head out to the alpine lakes, with crystal-clear water and breathtaking views, the easiest thing to do is to catch a Post Bus from the railway station or from Mirabellplatz. All kinds of water sports are on offer at the lakes, including wind-surfing, water skiing, sailing, kayaking and fishing.

The Alpentherme water park in Bad Hofgastein has everything from saunas and slides to beautiful outdoor pools with a panoramic view of the Alps (www.alpentherme.com/en; Sun–Wed 9am–9pm, Thu–Sat 9am–10pm).

CYCLING

Salzburg has been named Austria's most bike-friendly city. There are scenic cycle paths everywhere along the river, through Nonntal to Leopoldskron, Mülln and Anif (Hellbrunn). A few tips: stick to the cycle paths, know your hand signals, and be aware of other cyclists who tend to overtake at great speed. In Salzburg, it is not a legal obligation to wear a helmet, though it is much safer to do so. At night you must use front and rear lights. For pedestrians: do not walk on the cycle paths; when you hear a bell ringing, watch out, and move out of the way. If your hotel or hostel does not offer free bike loan, see page 116 for bike hire details.

HIKING

Salzburg and its surrounding area offer all levels of hiking. A good city walk goes from Mülln, over the Mönchsberg, through town and finishes off on the Kapuzinerberg. For something out of town but not too demanding, try the Gaisberg (to the east), which has a road all the way to the top. You can walk parallel with it, which makes finding the way easy. The view from the top of Gaisberg is breathtaking. If you want to push yourself and get away from the city, the Untersberg is perfect. Really adventurous types will find plenty of trekking routes in the Salzkammergut. Make sure you have an idea of the weather and save your hikes for clear days. You should buy a hiking guide that details rest huts and routes along the trails.

SALZBURG FOR CHILDREN

The best attractions for children are Hellbrunn Palace with its water fountains and zoo, the Open Air Museum in Grossgmain, Salzburg's fabulous Toy Museum with creative play areas, and the Natural History Museum. The latter is interactive, so even though the descriptions are in German, children can still get involved. Ice skating takes place all year round in the Volksgarten and during the Christmas season on Mozartplatz. Salzburg Marionette Theatre in Schwarzstrasse 24 is 100 years old and has never failed to attract children. Children are also thrilled by the Krampus runs in the first week of December. Summer brings swimming (pools supervised by lifeguards), cycling and street theatre. Outside the city, try the Alpentherme water park in Bad Hofgastein and the Forest Adventure Park in Anif.

CALENDAR OF EVENTS

For the most up-to-date information and comprehensive listings of events, contact the tourist information office (see page 132), follow posters and billboards around the city or check the official Salzburg travel guide at www.salzburg.info/en.

January New Year's Eve festivities continue through the night, with fireworks, live music and waltzing on Residenzplatz. Ball season is in full swing. *Mozartwoche* (Mozart Week; www.mozarteum.at/en/concerts/mozart-week) at the end of January sees 10 days of performances of Mozart's music.

February Carnival season ends with *Faschingsdienstag* (Shrove Tuesday), when fancy dress and partying take over the city.

March–April The *Osterfestspiele* (Easter Festival; www.osterfestspiele-salzburg.at/en) is celebrated with opera productions and orchestral performances over 10 days.

May The alternating *Biennale Salzburg* and *Aspekte Festival* are international forums of contemporary classical music. Baroque music is performed during the four-day *Salzburger Pfingstfestspiele* (Whitsun Festival; www.salzburgerfestspiele.at/whitsun).

June Midsummer festivals take place on the longest day of the year; beacons are lit on the highest peaks throughout Austria.

June–July The *SommerSzene* festival celebrates modern dance, with dancers and choreographers from all over the world.

July–August *Salzburger Festspiele* (Salzburg Festival; www.salzburgerfestspiele.at/summer) begins during the second half of July and continues until the end of August, commemorating the music of Mozart and other great composers.

September Harvest festivals take place throughout Salzburg province, with church services, craft and farmers' markets.

October–November Salzburg Culture Days *(Kulturtage)* is a four-week festival of opera and classical music, second only to the *Salzburger Festspiele*.

November The Christmas markets begin at the end of November.

December Christmas concerts take place throughout the illuminated city.

EATING OUT

Salzburg has a strong tradition of dining out. The oldest eatery in the city bears witness to this: St Peter Stidtskulinarium was established as a tavern by the monks of St Peter's in 803. You will often see whole families gathered around a restaurant table, or large groups of friends out celebrating a special occasion. Meals are not hurried and it is not unusual for people to spend a whole evening in a restaurant relishing a hefty three-course meal, with beer and wine flowing freely.

Summer is the time for eating outdoors. Many restaurants have gardens or, at the very least, tables on the pavement. Remember, however, that Salzburg is near the Alps and that

Stopping for a lunch of bread, cheese and meat

even in summer you might want a jumper or jacket.

WHAT TO EAT

Austrian cuisine is still more seasonal than in many other countries, especially regarding fruit, vegetables and herbs. Markets with fresh produce from the area play an essential part in the culture of home and especially restaurant cooking. Although the choice of fresh and packed products has widened immensely, you might not find the extreme array of convenience foods found in some supermarkets in the Anglo-Saxon world.

Salzburg has collected influences from all over Europe, especially the Austro-Hungarian Empire and, more recently, has been inspired by international cuisine. The Turks brought coffee and the coffee culture to Austria during the siege of Vienna in the 17th century; Gulasch and salamis come from the Hungarian part of the Austro-Hungarian Empire and some people even claim that the Schnitzel originated in Italy.

Local delicacies

Salzburg specialities include the ubiquitous Salzburger Nockerl (a very rich dessert made of fruit and soft meringue) and the savoury delicacies Kaspressknödel (a bread dumpling flavoured with cheese) and Fleischkrapfen (deep-fried pasties with a meat filling).

Meat

Traditionally, Austrian food has evolved around meat. Pork is the most popular item on the menu, closely followed by beef. Two of the classic meat dishes are Schweinsbraten (roast pork) and Zwiebelrostbraten (roast beef with gravy and onions). If you are a hungry carnivore and find it difficult to make up your mind, a Grillteller (mixed grill) is a good choice for sharing.

Vegetables

Vegetables are beginning to play a more important role as main dishes. As side dishes you will enjoy a lot of seasonal varieties. If you are here in the summer or autumn, the wild mushrooms (Pilze) are wonderful. In winter, pumpkins and root vegetables come into their own; Schwarzwurzel (black salsify) and Kohlrabi (a member of the cabbage family) are among the most popular. Finding good vegetarian food in Austria used to be a hopeless cause, but now nearly all restaurants offer a vegetarian alternative. There are also several vegetarian eateries (see pages 107, 110, 112). Organically grown produce is very popular here and you will find several restaurants and shops offering Bio produce.

Seasonal specialities

No matter what time of year you visit Salzburg, there is always some seasonal speciality on offer. In spring and early summer it's asparagus; in late summer it's Eierschwammerl (chanterelle mushrooms); in autumn it's game; in November it's goose; and at Christmas it is mulled wine and roast chestnuts. Austrians do not have a typical Christmas meal. Here it is traditional to eat fish on Christmas Eve, but steak or any other special treat are also options. Gingerbread and Christmas biscuits (Kekse) are the sweet specialities. On New Year's Eve, a fondue with either cheese or meat is a typical dish as it makes for a genial atmosphere around the table.

Bread and cheese

If you are looking for a snack or a light lunch, the wonderful dark Austrian breads are perfect to enjoy with a plate of Austrian cheeses or Speck (a dry-smoked bacon). There are many different types of cheese, ranging from strong-flavoured hard mountain cheeses to more gently flavoured soft cheese dips and spreads.

Marillenknödel are apricot dumplings

Desserts

During the hardships of World War II, people had to make do with the ingredients available to them. This has led to a love of desserts made from eggs, flour and milk. Many of the sweet dumplings, cakes and pancake-type dishes stem from these times. Although made from the simplest of ingredients, they can all be extremely delicious.

Coffee and cakes

The city is awash with cafés of all styles, and anybody spending a few days here will see that they play an important role in the social life of Salzburg's citizens. Nobody is in a hurry. The coffee-house culture means that you can sit over one cup of coffee, reading the café's newspapers and magazines, for as long as you want. This is just as well, as the first glance at the menu will reveal that coffee is not simply coffee. There

Apfelstrudel

are many types to choose from. All coffee served is made with espresso machines (the only time you might be served filter coffee is with breakfast in your hotel). The following list should help when choosing.

Verlängerter: A 'normal' cup of coffee made with one portion of espresso to two portions of water.

Espresso: One portion of espresso mixed with one of water.

Cappuccino: One part espresso to one of warm milk and one of whisked milk.

Latte macchiato: A double espresso in a large cup or glass topped with steamed milk and froth.

Melange: One portion of coffee, two measures of water and hot milk.

Einspänner: One portion of black coffee served in a tall glass with whipped cream (Schlagobers) and icing sugar on top.

Fiaker: A single espresso served in a glass with a dash of rum.

You will also notice that you will be served a small glass of tap water with your coffee. This is a tradition that was brought in by the Turks. Their coffee was (and still is) famously 'sludgy', so it was normal to serve a glass of water with which to wash down the grounds. Nowadays this is no longer necessary, but the tradition has remained.

Of course, coffee is not the sole focus of these places – an amazing array of cakes and buns is on offer. Choosing a cake can be quite daunting when faced with so many different, delicious-looking cream cakes, fruit flans, biscuits and other sweet delights. The most famous are Sachertorte (a chocolate cake) and Apfelstrudel (apples and raisins wrapped in thin layers of pastry). But there are many others to tempt you. The Cremeschnitte is a cream slice; Topfen is cream curd used in many cakes that are often topped with seasonal fruits or berries; Linzertorte is a tart with jam and nuts. Mandeln (almonds) are also used in many biscuits and cakes; a particularly good one is Bienenstich (literally 'bee sting'), a cake base filled with whipped cream and almonds with honey on top. A wonderfully gooey biscuit is the Florentiner (nuts and candied fruit covered in chocolate).

WHAT TO DRINK

Salzburg is split between the beer and the wine lovers, and both are well catered for.

Beer

With three locally brewed beers on offer – Stiegl, Kaiser and Augustiner – all with long histories, you will almost certainly find a beer to your taste. You should try the Weissbier at least once. This is a cloudy beer as the yeast has not been entirely brewed out (though you can also get a clear variety). It comes in a light and dark form, with the dark version being somewhat sweet. Zwickelbier is another slightly cloudy beer, an unfiltered lager. Bockbier is available at certain times of year, usually Christmas and Easter, and is a stronger special brew which should be handled with care – perhaps start with just a Pfiff (0.2 litres) to test the effect. The beer-garden culture is alive in the summer, and sitting in one of the leafy gardens, enjoying a beer or two, is a wonderful way to spend an evening.

Salzburg's taverns or Gasthäuser are an excellent combination of beer-hall and restaurant. You will often find some of the best Austrian food served in these establishments at very reasonable prices. For the most part they are traditional old taverns that have retained their wooden interiors and are cool in summer and cosy in winter.

Wine

If you have never tried Austrian wines, then the wine bars and restaurants in Salzburg are a good place to start. Although

⊘ AUSTRIAN FAST FOOD

It is hard to miss the usual fast-food outlets in Austria, but the international brand names are popular mainly with youngsters and tourists. True Austrian fast food comes in the form of the Würstlstand (sausage stand). These are scattered all over the city and you can usually find at least one open at any time of night or day. Sausages are available in all shapes and sizes, including Weisswurst from Munich, Frankfurters (hot dogs), Bosna (served with mustard, curry powder, ketchup and onions in a roll) and Käsekrainer (contains pieces of cheese).

this is not a wine-growing region, wines from Styria, Burgenland and Lower Austria are all worth trying. After the Austrian wine scandal in the 1980s, sales of Austrian wine plummeted. Many winegrowers had to lift their game, and now produce extremely high-quality wines in order to prove that most of the Austrian vineyards should be taken seriously. Both the red and white wines are very palat-

Steins of beer at the Augustiner Brewery

able and the most common are: Grüner Veltliner, a light, dry, crisp white wine; Welschriesling, a fresh, fruity white wine; Zweigelt, a full-bodied dry red; and Blauer Burgunder (Pinot Noir), a fruity, soft red. If you do not know what to choose, your waiter will be happy to recommend a good bottle.

When in Austria in the late summer and early autumn, you should try Sturm. This is grape juice which is still fermenting and has about 4 percent alcohol and is very refreshing. The white variety tends to be drier than the red one.

Another Austrian speciality is Schnaps. This is a strong, clear spirit produced using a variety of different fruits. The most commonly available types are Obstler, made from apples and pears, Marillenschnaps, made from apricots, and Vogelbeer, made from rowan berries. Try one after dinner as a digestif. They are also commonly used as cure-alls in Austrian households.

Soak up the coffee house culture when in Salzburg

TO HELP YOU ORDER...

Do you have a table for two/four? **Haben Sie einen Tisch für zwei/vier Personen, bitte?**

Could we have the menu? **Die Speisekarte, bitte?**

I/we would like... **Ich hätte/Wir hätten gern ...**

Could we have the bill, please? **Bezahlen, bitte.**

...AND READ THE MENU

Auflauf soufflé or a dish baked with cheese on top

Backhendl chicken sautéed in egg and breadcrumbs

Bauernschmaus meat with dumplings and sauerkraut

Blaukraut red cabbage

Blunzn black pudding

Bosna spicy sausages in a roll with onions, curry powder, mustard and ketchup

Brot bread

Buchteln/Wuchteln yeast buns filled with jam
Debreziner spicy Hungarian sausage
Eierschwammerl chanterelle mushrooms
Fleischlaberl meat rissoles
Frittatensuppe clear soup with sliced pancakes
Gefüllte paprika stuffed peppers
Germknödel big, fluffy yeast dumplings with poppy seeds
  (and custard)
Griessnockerlsuppe semolina dumpling soup
Gugelhupf Viennese sponge cake
Kaiserschmarrn pancake served with raisins and apple
  sauce
Kartoffelsalat potato salad
Kasspatzln pasta with cheese and fried onions
Knödel flour, potato or yeast dumpling
Krautsalat shredded white cabbage salad with caraway
  seeds
Marillenknödel apricot dumpling
Palatschinken pancakes with various fillings
Ribisel red or blackcurrants
Rostbraten pot roast
Salzburger Nockerl dessert with sponge cake, fruit and
  soft meringue
Schinkenfleckerl baked noodles with ham
Schwammerlsuppe mushroom soup
Schweinsbraten roast pork
Tafelspitz boiled beef
Topfenknödel dumpling made with curd
Wienerschnitzel veal or pork escalope fried in
  breadcrumbs
Zigeunerschnitzel pork escalope in paprika sauce
Zwiebelrostbraten beef steak with fried onions

PLACES TO EAT

We have used the following symbols to give an idea of the price for a three-course evening meal for one, excluding drinks and tips:

€€€ over 45 euros
€€ 20–45 euros
€ below 20 euros

OLD TOWN

Restaurants

Carpe Diem Finest Fingerfood €€–€€€ *Getreidegasse 50, tel: 848 800*, www.carpediemfinestfingerfood.com. Finger food at its finest, plus an abundance of other choices on the restaurant and dessert menus. Very stylish decor. Menus change monthly. Daily 8.30am–midnight.

Da Pippo €€ *Alter Markt 2, tel: 843 861*, www.dapippo.at. Superb Italian food with a buffet of cold starters and occasional live piano music while you eat. Located on the first floor overlooking Alter Markt; in the summer they have tables down in the square. Daily from 11.30am.

Goldener Hirsch €€€ *Getreidegasse 37, tel: 808 4861*, www.goldenerhirsch. com. This famous restaurant in the very elegant hotel of the same name specialises in fine Austrian cuisine. Antique artwork and traditional decor create a relaxing atmosphere in the vaulted hall, where a farrier once used to work. Over the years it has won numerous accolades for its food and is the place to go for a special occasion. Daily noon–2.30pm, 6.30–9.30pm.

Goldener Kugel €€ *Judengasse 3, tel: 2653 820*. Reasonably priced local food, like the Schnitzel or Apfelstrudel, in a traditional gasthaus setting in the middle of the historic city centre. Daily 10am–11pm.

Humboldt Stubn €–€€ *Gstättengasse 4–6, tel: 843 171*. A traditional restaurant and bar with an international menu and many Austrian specialities. Humboldt offers some vegetarian alternatives and excellent lunch deals. In summer there is a large, shady terrace. Daily 11am–3am.

Il Sole €€ *Gstättengasse 15, tel: 843 284*. Next to the entrance to the Mönchsberg lift, this Italian restaurant has friendly, efficient service and good pasta and pizzas (with vegetarian options) at very reasonable prices. Look out for the daily specials. Daily 11.30am–3.30pm, 5.30–11.30pm, closed Tue in spring and autumn.

Maredo €€ *Judengasse 5–7, tel: 843 894*, www.maredo.at. Fast and friendly service in this brightly lit steak restaurant, which is a perfect place to taste beef, pork or lamb Argentinian-style. The Maredo takes pride in the opulent salad buffet, which is a good choice for vegetarians, though not the only one. Daily 11.30am–11.30pm.

My Indigo € *Rudolfskai 8 (plus three other outlets in Salzburg), tel: 843 480*. These small fast-food establishments are excellent if you want a quick snack during the day while sightseeing. They offer Thai and vegetarian cuisine and delicious sweets. Some locations have indoor seating. Daily.

O'Malley's Irish Pub €€ *Rudolfskai 16, tel: 849 258*, www.omalleyssalzburg. com. The atmosphere, food, drink and entertainment of a real Irish pub in the heart of Salzburg. Mon–Thu and Sun 8pm–late, Fri–Sat 8pm–4am.

Paul Stube €€ *Herrengasse 16, tel: 843 220, 433 3203*. Situated in one of the cobbled alleys below the fortress, this is an old, traditional restaurant serving Austrian food. It fills up quickly, so it might be wise to reserve a table in advance. Pretty garden in the summer, too. Mon–Sat from 5pm.

Triangel €€ *Wiener-Philharmoniker-Gasse 7, tel: 842 229*, www.triangel-salzburg.co.at. A cosy, tavern-style restaurant close to the Festival Halls, popular with locals and visiting artists alike. Photographs of famous singers and conductors create an international ambience. Spacious outdoor seating in summer (200 places). Tue–Sat 11.30am–10pm.

Zipfer Bierhaus €€ *Universitätsplatz 19/Siegmund-Hafner-Gasse 12, tel: 840 745*, www.zipfer-bierhaus.at. In a 14th-century building where Nannerl (Mozart's sister) lived for almost 30 years, this traditional tavern serves Austrian food and beer in beer-hall style with a long line of hand pumps for the beers. The decor of antlers is quaintly traditional. Not many houses had their own well in the basement (still accessible) securing the water supply. Mon–Sat 10am–midnight; kitchen until 10pm.

Zirkelwirt €€ *Pfeifergasse 14, tel: 842 796.* An Austrian tavern with an international twist in the corner of Papagenoplatz. Fabulous meals at affordable prices. Also a pleasant place for just a coffee or beer. Daily 11am–midnight.

Zum Mohren €€ *Judengasse 9/Rudolfskai 20, tel: 840 680,* www.zummohren.at. A unique restaurant in Salzburg serving three wildly different cuisines: Austrian, Italian and Indian. Near the river, with the 13th-century town wall part of the building, it offers good lunchtime deals and friendly service. Daily 11am–11pm.

Zum Wilden Mann €€ *Getreidegasse 20 (passage to Griesgasse), tel: 841 787.* Long wooden tables to share with the locals. The menu is Austrian and the portions are huge in this Gasthaus dating back to 1884. The Schnitzel are great fare to be enjoyed with local beer and Austrian wines. Mon–Sat 11am–9pm.

Zwettler's €€ *Kaigasse 3, tel: 844 199,* www.zwettlers.com. Delicious typical Austrian dishes, decently priced, served in a traditional Austrian decor. Seasonal menus are worth trying too. Tue–Sat 11.30am–1am, Sun 11.30am–midnight.

Cafés

Afro Café *Bürgerspitalplatz 5, tel: 844 888,* www.afrocafe.at. In a very central location at the end of Griesgasse, Afro Café serves African specialities, from aromatic coffees and teas to mouthwatering snacks, breakfasts, salads, soups and tapas in a colourful, fresh interior inspired by the African continent. Interesting wines from South Africa as well as Austria. Mon–Thu 9am–11pm, Fri–Sat 9am–midnight, Sun only during Salzburg Festival weeks and Advent.

Fürst *Alter Markt/Brodgasse 13, tel: 843 7590*, www.original-mozart-kugel.com. The place where the famous Mozartkugel was invented. A busy little café with great cakes, coffees and ice creams and a huge selection of newspapers and magazines to choose from while you relax between sightseeing expeditions. Mon–Sat 8am–8pm, Sun 9am–8pm.

Mozart Café *Getreidegasse 22, tel: 843 958*, www.cafemozartsalzburg.at. The best place to try Salzburger Nockerl or other delicious Austrian desserts with your afternoon coffee. Also very good lunches, including vegetarian dishes. Mon–Sat 8am–9pm, Sun 9am–9pm.

Niemetz *Herbert-von-Karajan-Platz 11, tel: 843 367*. With an enviable location next to the Festival Halls, this café is a favourite with concert-goers and is full of festival memorabilia. You can sit over coffee, cake and a newspaper for as long as you like. Mon–Sat 10am–6pm.

Tomaselli *Alter Markt 9, tel: 844 4880,* www.tomaselli.at. Dating from the early 18th century, Tomaselli is the oldest café in Salzburg. It is worth a visit to see the traditionally dressed waitresses wheeling trolleys full of cakes, but it is not the cheapest or friendliest café in town. Mon–Sat 7am–7pm, Sun 8am–7pm, during Salzburg festival season until 9pm.

NEW TOWN
Restaurants

Andreas Hofer € *Steingasse 65, tel: 872 769*. Located in one of the oldest lanes of town, through which farmers and salt merchants used to approach Salzburg with horse and cart. This old pub has the rustic ambience of times gone by. Speck (dry-smoked ham), Knödel (dumplings) and cheese are menu classics at 'Andi Hofer' – and provide a good basis for an evening of wine tasting. Mon–Sat and holidays 6pm–1am.

Bangkok €€ *Bayerhamerstrasse 33, tel: 873 688*. Excellent Thai food in a quiet little restaurant with attentive, friendly service and reasonable prices. Tue–Sun 11.30am–2.30pm and 5.30–11pm.

Beccofino €€ *Rupertgasse 7, tel: 879 878*. Italian specialities, including pizza, pasta, fish and meat dishes. Gluten- and lactose-free pasta on demand. The restaurant also serves Halal meat to Muslim customers. Mon–Fri 11am–2pm and 5–9.30pm, Sat–Sun and holidays 5–9.30pm.

Die Weisse/Sudwerk €€ *Rupertgasse 10, tel: 872 246*. This restaurant incorporates a small brewery that makes its own Weissbier and serves excellent Austrian cuisine. Different rooms cater for different tastes and styles. The musical events are highly popular. Mon–Sat 10am–2am.

Maier's €€ *Steingasse 61, tel: 879 379*. This small reputable restaurant serves tasty international cuisine in a cosy atmosphere. Warm meals until 10pm. Tue–Sat from 6pm.

Taj Mahal €€ *Bayerhamerstrasse 13 (corner of Lasserstrasse), tel: 882 010*, www.restaurant-tajmahal.com. A popular Indian restaurant serving good curries in a relaxed atmosphere. British travellers should not expect the food to be as spicy as in some UK Indian restaurants, as Austrians prefer their curries to be on the mild side. Daily 11.30am–2pm, 5.30–10pm (closed for lunch Sat).

Zum Fidelen Affen €€ *Priesterhausgasse 8, tel: 877 361*, www.fideleraffe. at. Dark panelling, wooden tables and floors give this Gastwirtschaft a warm, welcoming atmosphere. Good food, friendly service and popular with locals. Mon–Sat 5pm–midnight, warm meals until 11pm.

Cafés and bars

Bellini's *Mirabellplatz 4, tel: 871 385*. An Italian café close to the Mirabell Gardens. Serves Italian coffee and snacks. Outdoor seating. Mon–Sat 8am–1am, Sun 10am–1am.

Café Bazar *Schwarzstrasse 3, tel: 874 278*, www.cafe-bazar.at. Slightly expensive, but with a lovely terrace overlooking the river. The art deco interior has been elegantly renovated. Sit and watch the world go by as all the famous literary figures in Salzburg did. Mon–Sat 7.30am–7.30pm, Sun 9am–6pm (7.30am–11pm July–Aug).

Café Classic *Makartplatz 8, tel: 882 700*. Located in Mozart's town-house, this café is very much along the lines of a Viennese coffee house. Wonderful breakfasts, cakes and frothy coffee. Mon–Sat 8am–7.30pm.

Café Confiserie Sacher *Schwarzstrasse 5–7, tel: 88977,* www.sacher. com. A sister of the famous Café Sacher in Vienna and 'inventor' of the chocolate cake of the same name. Treat yourself to a wonderful moist slice of this cake, or order a meal. In summer, there is a terrace on the river. Daily 7.30am–11pm.

Daimler's Bar & Late-Night Grill *Giselakai 17, tel: 873 967.* A lively, popular bar overlooking the river. Serves delicious burgers, salads, sandwiches, finger food and steaks into the small hours. Sun–Thu 7.30pm–2am, Fri–Sat 7.30pm–4am.

Fingerlos *Franz-Josef-Strasse 9, tel: 874 213*. Best ever coffee and cakes, all made on the premises. This is a popular place for breakfast too, if not the cheapest. The decor is modern and bright and in summer there are tables on the pavement. Tue–Sun 7.30am–7.30pm.

Steinterrasse *Giselakai 3–5, tel: 874 346 700*. Part of a trendy hotel, this is one of the most popular places in Salzburg and a great location for people-watching. The terrace affords a panoramic view of the city and in the evenings you can get what are considered to be the best cocktails in town. Sun–Thu 7am–midnight, Fri–Sat until 1am.

BORDERS AND SUBURBS

Restaurants

Augustiner Bräu Kloster Mülln € *Lindhofstrasse7/Augustinergasse 4, tel: 431 246,* www.augustinerbier.at. Genuine beer-hall atmosphere in a brewery founded by Augustinian monks on the northern slope of the Mönchsberg. Wonderful beer, beautiful garden and plenty of snacks to choose from. You can even bring your own picnic. Mon–Fri 3–11pm, Sat–Sun and holidays 2.30–11pm.

Bärenwirt €€ *Müllner Hauptstrasse 8, tel: 422 404.* A traditional restaurant serving Austrian cuisine, vegetarian and wholegrain food. There has been a restaurant on this site for over 350 years. Daily 11am–11pm, warm meals 11.30am–2pm, 5.30–9.30pm.

Esszimmer €€€ *Müllner Hauptstrasse 33, tel: 870 899,* www.restaurant-esszimmer.jimdo.com. Fine dining in a lovely location. This one-Michelin-star restaurant has an excellent reputation (and correspondingly high prices). Its relaxed atmosphere makes it a popular place. Vegetarians are well catered for. There is a quiet garden in summer. Tue–Sat noon–2pm, 6.30–9.30pm (open Mon during Salzburg Festival weeks).

Hotel Friesacher €€ *Hellbrunner Strasse 17, Anif, tel: 468 977,* www.friesacher.com. Friesacher has an excellent reputation as one of the best traditional restaurants serving Austrian food, wine and beer. Although slightly out of town in Anif, the hotel restaurant is worth making the journey for, particularly if you are visiting Hellbrunn.

Ikarus €€€ *Hangar-7, Wilhelm-Spazier-Strasse 7a, tel: 219 70,* www.hangar-7.com. This is a restaurant with a difference. Enjoy a first-class meal with a view of the collection of vintage aircraft and racing cars in Hangar-7, owned by Red Bull boss Dietrich Mateschitz. Top guest chefs from around the world spend a month at a time cooking up delights. Reservations essential. Daily 7–10pm, Thu–Sun also noon–2pm.

Irodion €€ *Neutorstrasse 34, tel: 842 918.* Probably Salzburg's best Greek restaurant. It is very popular and reservations are recommended. All your favourite Greek dishes served in warm and welcoming surroundings. There is a lovely garden in the summer. Daily 11am–3pm, 5.30pm–midnight.

Krimpelstätter Augustiner Braugasthof €€ *Müllner Hauptstrasse 31, tel: 432 274.* Close to the Müllner church is this traditional tavern with a beer garden serving authentic Austrian dishes. Schottnsuppe (a cream soup with curd) and spinach dumplings are vegetarian delights. Very popular with the festival crowd. Tue–Sat 11am–midnight.

Magazin €€€ *Augustinergasse 13, tel: 841 584 20*. Mönchsberg is the dramatic backdrop to this 21st-century restaurant – its design as creative as the cuisine, though with a pleasant classic touch. Under the same roof you will find a shop with select kitchen utensils and wines. Tue–Sat from 11.30am.

Prosecco €€€ *Nonntaler Hauptstrasse 55, tel: 834 017*. A restaurant serving fine Italian fare in a nice ambiance. Mon–Sat 11.30am–2.30pm, 6pm–midnight (closed Sat lunch).

Riedenburg €€€ *Neutorstrasse 31, tel: 830 815*. This is considered by some to be the best restaurant in Salzburg. Try the three-course lunch menu for less than €20. The wine list is also exquisite. Reservations recommended. Tue–Sat noon–2pm, 6–10pm, daily during Salzburg Festival weeks.

Wastlwirt €€ *Rochusgasse 15, Maxglan, tel: 822 162*. Located in a quiet corner, not far from the city centre, this traditional tavern is wonderfully cosy with lots of wood and a leafy, shady garden. Mon–Fri 11am–midnight, Sat 4pm–midnight.

Cafés

Carpe Diem Lounge *Hangar-7, Wilhelm-Spazier-Strasse 7a, tel: 219 70*, www.hangar-7.com. An elegantly furnished café housed under the glass dome of Hangar-7. Enjoy your coffee while watching the goings-on in the museum through the glass wall. Daily 9am–5pm.

Wiener Café Herbert *Nonntaler Hauptstrasse 87, tel: 820 7609*. Typical Viennese café with good home-made cakes. Hot meals served between 11am and 2pm. Mon–Sat 8.30am–6pm, Sun 9.30am–6pm.

A–Z TRAVEL TIPS

A SUMMARY OF PRACTICAL INFORMATION

A Accommodation ___ **115**
Airport ___ **115**
B Bicycle hire ___ **116**
Budgeting for your trip ___ **116**
C Camping ___ **117**
Car hire ___ **118**
Climate ___ **118**
Clothing ___ **119**
Crime and safety ___ **119**
D Disabled travellers ___ **119**
Driving ___ **120**
E Electricity ___ **122**
Embassies and consulates ___ **123**
Emergencies ___ **123**
G Gay and lesbian travellers ___ **123**
Getting there ___ **124**
Guides and tours ___ **125**
H Health and medical care ___ **126**

L Language ___ **126**
Lost property ___ **126**
M Maps ___ **127**
Media ___ **127**
Money ___ **127**
O Opening times ___ **128**
P Police ___ **129**
Post offices ___ **129**
Public holidays ___ **130**
R Religion ___ **130**
T Telephones ___ **131**
Tickets ___ **131**
Time zones ___ **131**
Tipping ___ **132**
Toilets ___ **132**
Tourist information ___ **132**
Transport ___ **133**
V Visas and entry requirements ___ **133**
W Websites ___ **134**
Y Youth hostels ___ **135**

A

ACCOMMODATION (see also Camping, Youth hostels and Recommended hotels on page 136)

Salzburg has a wide selection of accommodation, including the usual chain hotels such as Radisson, Sheraton, Mercure and Dorint, but also offers privately run hotels that tend to be friendlier and more characterful.

For most of the year it is not necessary to book accommodation in advance, but during peak times (Easter, July, August and December) advance reservations are essential. The Salzburg Tourist Office website, www.salzburg.info, offers an online booking service, in English as well as German. The Tourist Office also publishes a booklet of accommodation every year, though this is not a complete listing of all the hotels and guesthouses in the city.

If you have not booked somewhere to stay before you arrive, the tourist information offices at the railway station and on Mozartplatz can assist with finding accommodation.

Pensionen are the equivalent of guesthouses or bed and breakfasts, and are less expensive than hotels.

a guesthouse **eine Pension**
a single/double room **ein Einzelzimmer/Doppelzimmer**
with/without bath (shower) **mit/ohne Bad (Dusche)**
What's the rate per night? **Was kostet eine Übernachtung?**

AIRPORT

Salzburg's airport, W.A. Mozart, www.salzburg-airport.com, is located on the western edge of the city. The airport is small, but offers all the usual facilities: restaurant, bar, banks, shops, cafés and a newsagent.

There are regular buses (€2.60 for a single ticket) to the railway station (direct) and the city centre (change of bus). The journey to the station takes approximately 30 minutes. There is also a taxi rank directly outside the arrivals terminal. All car-hire offices are across the road in the multistorey car park.

Arrivals are through Terminal I, but in winter the ski charter flights depart from Terminal II.

B

BICYCLE HIRE

Salzburg is considered Austria's most bike-friendly community. It has a superb network of cycle paths around the city and along the riverbanks. A number of hotels offer free bike loan. If yours does not, there are plenty of bike-hire shops (about €6 for 2 hours, €10 for 4 hours, €15 for a day). **Bikepalast Salzburg** (tel: 633 030) has an office at Bayerhamerstrasse. The Bike Map of Salzburg is available at www.salzburg.info.

The Mozartradweg (Mozart Bike Trail) runs from the city through the Salzburg Lake District (Salzkammergut) on to Bavaria and its lakes, before ending at Berchtesgaden, near Hitler's former holiday retreat (see page 70). The route stretches about 450km (280 miles) and is primarily flat, with just a few hills along the way. It's ideal for families. Salzburg tourist offices will provide trail maps (see page 132).

BUDGETING FOR YOUR TRIP

The currency in Austria is the euro. To give you a rough guide of how much things cost, the following is a list of average prices:

Drinks: non-alcoholic drinks in bars and restaurants around €2.50–3.50, 0.5l beer €3.50–4, 0.125l wine €4 upwards.

Entertainment: cinema ticket around €10, entrance into a nightclub or disco from around €5.

Hotels: a double room with breakfast will cost €160 and upwards per night in a five-star hotel, between €65 and €80 in a two-star.

Meals: a three-course evening meal in a mid-range restaurant will cost between €25 and €35 per head, including a drink.

Museums: admission fees vary greatly; there are reductions for children and students. A Salzburg Card (see page 12) provides free admission to many museums.

Public transport: single tickets cost €2.60 if you buy them on the bus and €1.90 if you buy them in advance in a block of five from tobacconists or customer care centres. Day passes cost €5.70 if you buy them on the bus, €4 using a mobile phone or a vending machine and €3.80 if you buy in advance from tobacconists or customer care centres (https://salzburg-verkehr.at). Bus travel is included in the Salzburg Card.

Sightseeing: a *Fiaker* (horse-drawn carriage) trip for up to five people costs €185 for a 50-minute tour (www.fiaker-salzburg.at). A boat trip on the *Amadeus Salzburg* costs €15–29 for adults and €7.50–19 for children (www.salzburghighlights.at). If you join a Salzburg city guide for a guided group tour, it costs around €10 per person.

Tickets: concerts €10–60; Salzburger Landestheater €11–70; Marionette Theatre €20–37 for adults, €15 for children. Salzburg Festival (www.salzburgerfestspiele.at): tickets vary greatly in price according to the performance.

C

CAMPING

There are three campsites in the vicinity of Salzburg: Nord Sam (tel: 660 494, www.camping-nord-sam.com, open mid-Apr–early Dec, Christmas–early Jan); Camping Panorama Stadtblick (tel: 450 652, www.panorama-camping.at, open end Mar–early Nov, early Dec, late Dec–early Jan) and Camping Schloss Aigen (tel: 622 079, www.camping aigen.com, open May–Sept).

TRAVEL TIPS

CAR HIRE (see also Driving)

To explore Salzburg it is not necessary to have a car. It is easy to lose your bearings in the maze of one-way streets, and parking is expensive and very limited. However, should you need car hire for trips out of town, most of the major car hire companies have offices at the airport and will deliver cars to your hotel. Costs are around €70 for an economy class car for one day, €120 for a weekend.

For hiring a car, you need to be aged over 19, hold a driving licence, passport and one of the major credit cards. A fire and third-party liability insurance is mandatory and included in all rentals.

Europcar tel: 1866 161 633, www.europcar.at
Avis tel: 877 278, www.avis.at
Buchbinder tel: 0810 007 010, www.buchbinder-rent-a-car.at
Hertz tel: 876 674, www.hertz.at
Sixt tel: 977 424, www.sixt.at

> I'd like to rent a car **Ich möchte bitte ein Auto mieten**
> Tomorrow **für morgen**
> for one day/week **für einen Tag/für eine Woche**
> Please include full insurance. **Mit Vollkaskoversicherung, bitte.**

CLIMATE

Salzburg has a well-deserved reputation for being a rainy city and the watery weather even has a nickname: *Schnürlregen* (string-rain). It can rain for three seasons of the year, and in winter it snows instead. Salzburg can be quite cold in winter and stiflingly hot in summer. The best times of year for visiting the city in pleasant temperatures are spring and autumn. In spring the alpine flowers are in full bloom, and in autumn the colours of the forest are aglow. At these times the streets are not filled to bursting point with tourists. If you are looking for some romantic winter atmosphere, then December, when the Christmas Markets are in full swing, is also a good time, but much busier.

Below is a chart showing Salzburg's average temperatures and rainfall for the year:

	J	F	M	A	M	J	J	A	S	O	N	D
°C	1	4	11	16	20	24	25	24	21	15	8	2
°F	34	39	52	61	68	75	77	75	70	59	46	36
mm	54	49	41	52	73	110	134	108	81	67	53	46

CLOTHING

Whatever the time of year, it is always best to bring layers and something waterproof. It may be freezing cold outside in winter, but the buildings are all very well heated and insulated inside. There can be cold snaps in summer, so light jumpers or jackets will be useful.

Austrians dress casually for most occasions, but they do like to be smart when going to the theatre, opera, ballet or a ball. Evening dress is often worn to festival performances.

CRIME AND SAFETY

Salzburg is a very safe city. You do need to watch out for pickpockets in busy places (such as markets) and make sure you lock up your bicycle if you park it anywhere. Do not leave valuables in your car, and ensure that it is locked. In the event of theft or crime call 112 or 133 to get the nearest police station (*Polizeiwache*).

D

DISABLED TRAVELLERS

Salzburg Information has good website information (www.salzburg.

info/en/salzburg/barrier-free) and has published the free guide *Experience Barrier-Free Salzburg*, listing sights, hotels and places of interest with their level of wheelchair access. It includes a map and plenty of useful information for wheelchair users. Most of the buses in the city are accessible with a wheelchair, although some of the older ones are not.

DRIVING (See also Car hire)

If you are taking your car to Austria, you must have a valid driving licence, third-party insurance, car registration papers, a red warning triangle and a reflective high-visibility waistcoat in case of breakdown, and a first-aid kit. From 1st November to 15th April only cars with winter tyres are allowed to drive on roads with snow and ice (snow chains are recommended for the mountains).

For Austrian motorways you will require a toll sticker (*Vignette*), valid between 10 days and a year. They are sold at petrol stations, post offices and tobacconists.

---

driving licence **Führerschein**
car registration papers **Zulassungsschein**
Green Card **Grüne Karte**
Where's the nearest car park, please? **Wo ist der nächste Parkplatz, bitte?**
Can I park here? **Darf ich hier parken?**
Are we on the right road for ...? **Sind wir auf der richtigen Strasse nach ...?**
Check the oil/tyres/battery, please. **Öl/Reifen/Batterie prüfen, bitte.**
I've had a breakdown. **Ich habe eine Panne.**
There's been an accident. **Es ist ein Unfall passiert.**

Road conditions. The roads in Austria are very good on the whole. The north–south routes can get very busy at weekends in the summer, and in winter, when people are heading to and from the ski resorts. Information on road conditions and the traffic situation is available in English seven days a week 6am–8pm (tel: 0043-1 711 997).

Driving regulations. Austrians drive on the right. Here are some of the rules of the road that you might find useful:

It is compulsory to wear seatbelts in front and rear seats.

It is forbidden to use a hand-held mobile phone while driving.

Children under the age of 12 are not permitted to sit in the front.

It is forbidden to overtake on the right on the motorway.

Headlights must be switched on at all times.

The alcohol limit is 0.5 parts per thousand.

Speed limits. On motorways 130kmh (81mph) or 110kmh (68mph); on other roads 100kmh (62mph) or 80kmh (50mph); in built-up areas 50kmh (31mph).

Parking. It can be difficult to park in Salzburg. It is not permitted to park in the bus lanes during the stated times. For the blue parking bays you will need to display a ticket (machines are located nearby).

Breakdowns. There is a 24-hour breakdown service for motorways and main roads. The two Austrian motoring clubs are ÖAMTC (tel: 120, www.oeamtc.at) and ARBÖ (tel: 123, www.arboe.at).

Fuel and oil. There are plenty of petrol stations around Salzburg. Not all are open 24 hours, but those on the motorway and at the major entrances to the city are. Petrol, diesel and LPG are available.

Road signs. Most road signs employed in Austria are international, but here are some written signs you might come across:

Anfang (parking) start
Ausfahrt exit

Aussicht viewpoint
Bauarbeiten road works
Einbahnstrasse one way
Ende (parking) end
Fahrbahnwechsel change lanes
Fußgänger pedestrians
Gefahr danger
Geradeaus straight on
Glatteis icy roads
Halten verboten no stopping
Licht einschalten use headlights
Ortsende town ends
Parken erlaubt parking allowed
Rechts/links einbiegen turn right/left
Rollsplitt loose gravel
Sackgasse no through road
Spital hospital
Steinschlag falling stones
Umleitung detour
Vorfahrt priority
Vorsicht caution
Werktags von 7 bis 17 Uhr
  weekdays 7am to 5pm
Zufahrt gestattet entrance permitted

E

ELECTRICITY

Austrian plugs have two round pins, so an adapter is necessary if your
device has a British or US plug. The voltage is 220 volts.

EMBASSIES AND CONSULATES

Contact your consulate or embassy only for real emergencies, such as loss of a passport or all your money, a serious accident or trouble with the police. Citizens of most countries will have to contact their embassies in Vienna or a consulate in Munich. The honorary consulate in Salzburg is:

UK: Rainbergstrasse 3c, 5020 Salzburg, tel: 624 500.

EMERGENCIES (See also Crime and safety, and Police)

Normally, in the case of an emergency, your hotel receptionist will be happy to assist. If you do need to get hold of the emergency services yourself, the numbers are as follows:

Emergency (general): **112**

Police: **133**

Fire brigade: **122**

Ambulance, first aid: **144**

Emergency medical service: **141**

I need a doctor/dentist/ambulance. **Ich brauche einen Arzt/Zahnarzt/Krankenwagen.**

Fire! **Feuer!**

Help! **Hilfe!**

hospital **Spital**

police **Polizei**

G

GAY AND LESBIAN TRAVELLERS

The gay and lesbian scene in Salzburg is not very evident, though there is the gay-friendly Wolf-Dietrich hotel right in the city centre in Wolf-Dietrich-Strasse 7 and the hottest party spot for gays and lesbians,

Mexxx Gay Bar (www.mexxxgaybar.at), in Schallmooser Hauptstrasse 20. Four times a year HOSI Festival for gays and lesbians takes place at ArgeKultur, organised by the HOSI Homosexual Initiative in Salzburg (www.hosi.or.at), which also runs a gay bar in Gabelsbergerstrasse 26.

GETTING THERE

By air

Scheduled flights. There are regular flights year-round from several UK airports, and from Dublin, to Salzburg. Ryanair, www.ryanair.com, has daily flights to Salzburg from London Stansted, British Airways, www.britishairways.com, from London Heathrow and London Gatwick, and Easyjet, www.easyjet.com, weekly flights from London Gatwick, London Luton, Bristol and Liverpool and Norwegian, www.norwegian. com, from London Gatwick during skiing season.

Charter flights. During the summer and winter seasons there are charter flights from a number of UK and Republic of Ireland airports. These are normally sold on a seat-only basis unless you are booking a package. Many UK tour operators offer Salzburg as a city break. Check with your travel agent for details.

Via Munich. The choice of scheduled flights to Munich is much greater than to Salzburg. Munich is about 1.5–2 hours away from Salzburg by train (buy a Bayern Ticket from ticket machines at stations – this gives you all-day travel on regional trains within Bavaria and Salzburg) and 1.5 hours by car.

By car

Salzburg is a long drive from the UK and you should allow two days' travelling time. Although the German motorways are pretty good, they can get very busy over the summer months. The quickest route is via Ostende, Cologne, Stuttgart and Munich.

Comfortable motor rails/car trains run between Hamburg and Vienna via Munich. Contact Austrian Federal Railways (ÖBB) for details (www.oebb.at) or Deutsche Bahn (www.bahn.de).

By rail

There are regular train services from London St Pancras International to Salzburg via Paris and Munich. The journey takes about 16 hours. Sleepers and couchettes are available if booked in advance. Contact ÖBB (*see above*) for further information.

GUIDES AND TOURS

There are two major bus tour companies in Salzburg that offer guided tours of the city in English both by coach and on foot, and also to places of interest nearby: Salzburg Sightseeing Tours (tel: 881 616, www.salzburg-sightseeingtours.at) and Panorama Tours (tel: 883 2110, www.panoramatours.com). Both have *The Sound of Music* tours, which visit all the film locations in and around the city.

The local tourist office at Mozartplatz also organises guided tours on foot with English-speaking guides.

Outside the Residenz you will find a row of horse-drawn carriages awaiting customers. These are known as *Fiakers* and will take you through the old town at a leisurely pace (see page 37).

Boat trips on the Salzach aboard the *Amadeus Salzburg* are available between May and September. They leave at regular intervals from the Makartsteg (pedestrian bridge) in the Old Town and take you as far as Hellbrunn Castle and the zoo.

We'd like an English-speaking guide. **Wir möchten einen englisch sprachigen Fremdenführer.**

I need an English interpreter. **Ich brauche einen Dolmetscher für Englisch.**

How long will the ride take? **Wie lange dauert die Fahrt?**

What does it cost? **Was kostet es?**

H

HEALTH AND MEDICAL CARE

The health service in Salzburg is excellent. There are numerous medical facilities, including the *Unfallkrankenhaus* (Accident Hospital) on Dr-Franz-Rehrl-Platz 5 (tel: 65 800) and the *Krankenhaus und Konvent der Barmherzigen Brüder*, Kajetanerplatz 1 (tel: 80 880). The *Unfallkrankenhaus* is renowned for treating injured skiers. Austria and the UK have a reciprocal agreement as far as hospital treatment is concerned. UK citizens (and citizens of other EU countries) should obtain the European Health Insurance Card (EHIC) before travelling, available online at www.ehic.org.uk. This entitles them to reduced-cost, sometimes free, medical treatment. However, full travel insurance is still advised.

If you are taking prescription drugs, bring with you enough supply for the duration of your trip. The same drugs may not be available in Salzburg.

In order to buy any sort of medication, you will have to go to a chemist (*Apotheke*). Should you require a chemist outside normal opening times, there is usually a duty roster posted on the door of all chemists.

L

LANGUAGE

German is spoken in Austria. As Salzburg relies heavily on tourism, many of the people here speak at least a little English. Even so, you can try with a little German: *Entschuldigen Sie bitte* (Excuse me, please) is always appreciated. You could also ask, *Sprechen Sie Englisch?* (Do you speak English?), another good way to start. The *Berlitz German Phrase Book & Dictionary* covers most situations you may come across in Austria.

LOST PROPERTY

The city lost property office is on the ground floor of the town hall in Mirabell Palace, open Mon–Thu 7.30am–4pm, Fri 7.30am–1pm, tel: 8072 3580, fundamt@stadt-salzburg.at, www.fundamt.gv.at.

I've lost my passport/wallet/handbag. **Ich habe meinen Pass/meine Brieftasche/Handtasche verloren.**

MAPS

The tourist office and hotels have free street maps of Salzburg, which are detailed enough for walking around the centre. Bigger city maps are available from the tourist board and bookshops.

Maps of the bus routes can be picked up free in either the tourist information offices or from the railway station.

MEDIA

English-language newspapers are available at the airport, the railway station and some newsagents throughout the town. Most hotels also have a stock of the dailies. The English-language daily papers available in Salzburg are usually one day late. *Salzburger Nachrichten* (www.salzburg.com) is the leading regional daily. *Der Standard* (www.derstandard.at), Die Presse (www.diepresse.com) and *Kronen Zeitung* (www.krone.at) are the main national daily newspapers.

Most of the hotels in Salzburg have cable TV. If your hotel has satellite TV, you will probably have a greater choice of English-speaking channels.

MONEY

Currency. Austria's monetary unit is the euro. The euro is divided into 100 cents. Banknotes in denominations of 500, 100, 50, 20, 10 and 5 are in circulation. There are coins to the value of 1 and 2 euros, 50, 20, 5, 2 and 1 cents.

Changing money. You can exchange your money at any of the banks in the city. Hotels also offer money-exchange facilities, but their rates are not as good as those of the banks. All banks have ATM machines (cash-points); most of them accept UK debit cards. Bureaux de change are also scattered throughout the city. These have the advantage of being open after the banks have closed.

Credit cards. The major credit and debit cards are widely accepted in Austria, but smaller shops, bars and restaurants still do not accept them.

I want to change some pounds/dollars. **Ich möchte Pfund/ Dollar wechseln.**
Do you accept traveller's cheques? **Nehmen Sie Reiseschecks an?**
Do you have any change, please? **Haben Sie Kleingeld, bitte?**
Where's the nearest cashpoint, please? **Wo ist der nächste Geldautomat, bitte?**

O

OPENING TIMES

Shops. These can be divided into two categories when it comes to opening times. The first are the small shops in the shopping districts in town. These are mostly open from 9am until 6pm (some close for an hour or two at lunchtime) Mondays to Fridays and until 5pm on Saturdays. Supermarkets and shopping centres tend to be open from 9am until 7.30 or 8pm Mondays to Fridays and until 5pm on Saturdays. The only shops open on Sundays are those selling souvenirs.

Museums. These vary widely; for opening times check the individual

entries in the Where to Go section, or the website www.salzburg.info.
Banks. Mostly Mon–Fri 8am–12.30pm and 2–4.30pm, Thu until 5.30pm.
Chemists. Mostly Mon–Fri 8am–noon and 2pm–6pm, Sat 8am–noon.

P

POLICE (see also Crime and safety and Emergencies)

Police have blue uniforms with dark blue caps and carry guns. If you are
fined for a traffic offence, you are likely to be asked to pay on the spot.
Street parking in Salzburg is supervised by traffic wardens, who wear
dark blue trousers and white shirts.

The main police station is at Landespolizeikommando Salzburg, Alpenstrasse 88–90, 5020 Salzburg; tel: 059 13350.

In an emergency, contact the police on **112** or **133**.

> Where is the nearest police station, please? **Wo ist die
> nächste Polizeiwachstube, bitte?**

POST OFFICES

Salzburg's main post office is at Residenzplatz 9. Opening times are
Mon–Fri 8am–6pm. The post office in the station is open Mon–Fri
8am–7pm, Sat 9am–1pm. If you just need stamps, you can also buy
these from any tobacconist. Information on Austrian postal services
can be found at: www.post.at. Salzburg's post boxes are yellow.

> Express (special delivery) **Express/Eilbote**
> Airmail **Luftpost**
> Have you any mail for ...? **Haben Sie Post für...?**
> A stamp for this letter/postcard, please **Eine Marke für
> diesen Brief/diese Postkarte, bitte.**

PUBLIC HOLIDAYS

On public holidays in Austria all offices and banks, most shops and some restaurants are closed. Note that on Good Friday, a holiday for Protestants only, shops etc remain open. On 24 December (Christmas Eve) all theatres and cinemas are closed, and most shops and restaurants close at midday.

1 January *Neujahrstag* New Year's Day
6 January *Heilige Drei Könige* Epiphany
1 May *Tag der Arbeit* Labour Day
15 August *Maria Himmelfahrt* Assumption
26 October *Nationalfeiertag* National Holiday
1 November *Allerheiligen* All Saints' Day
8 December *Maria Empfängnis* Immaculate Conception
25 December *Weihnachten* Christmas Day
26 December *Stefanitag* Boxing Day
Movable dates:
Ostermontag Easter Monday
Christi Himmelfahrt Ascension Day
Pfingstmontag Whit Monday
Fronleichnam Corpus Christi

Are you open tomorrow? **Haben Sie morgen geöffnet?**

R

RELIGION

Most Austrians are Roman Catholics, but there are Protestant parishes everywhere and also Muslim communities. English-language Catholic services are held every Sunday at the Sacellum on Herbert-von-Karajan-Platz at 11.30am. Protestant services are held in the Christus Kirche, Schwarzstrasse 25, Sunday 9.30am.

The synagogue is at Lasserstrasse 8.

T

TELEPHONES

Try to avoid using the phone in your hotel room: hotels can charge well over the odds. The net coverage for mobile phones is excellent, making roaming possible. To buy a local SIM-card can work out cheaper for longer stays.

The international dialling code for Austria is 43, the code for Salzburg 0662 (leave off the 0 if calling from abroad). To make an international call from Austria, dial 00 and then the country code (44 for the UK, 1 for the USA and Canada) and again omit the first zero from your area code.

TICKETS

There are a number of ticket agencies in the city and all charge booking fees. The most central and best known is Salzburg Ticket Service, Mozartplatz 5 (tel: 840 310, www.salzburgticket.com).

Salzburg Festival. Tickets for the Salzburg Festival go on sale in November and can be applied for online at www.salzburgerfest spiele.at until the first week in January. Remaining tickets go on sale from April onwards. Ticket office: Herbert-von-Karajan-Platz 11 (tel: 804 5500).

Mozart Festival. Tickets for the Mozart Festival in January can be booked with the Stiftung Mozarteum (tel: 889 400, www.mozarteum.at).

Other events. Tickets for the Marionette Theatre can be booked directly with the box office or online (tel: 872 406, www.marionetten. at). The Mozart Dinner Concert can be booked with Salzburger Konzertgesellschaft at Getreidegasse 47 (tel: 828 695, www.salzburg-concerts.com), or at the box office before the start of a performance.

TIME ZONES

The time in Austria is Central European Time, which is one hour ahead of GMT. There is daylight saving time as in the UK, with the clocks going forward one hour at the end of March and back one hour at the end of October. The time differences are as follows:

New York	London	**Salzburg**	Jo'burg	Sydney	Auckland
6am	11am	**noon**	noon	8pm	10pm

TIPPING

In bars, restaurants and cafés it is customary to tip around 10 percent, even though a service charge is normally included. For smaller amounts, it is good practice to round up the bill. Although service charges are included in hotel bills, porters and maids do expect a tip. Tour guides, taxi drivers and hairdressers also rely heavily on the tips they receive.

TOILETS

There are many public toilets around the city, especially in the centre. There is usually a 50-cent charge for toilets with an attendant. Signs in toilets are *Damen* (ladies) and *Herren* (gents).

TOURIST INFORMATION

The **Salzburg Tourism Office** has a website in English: www.salzburg.info/en. This includes a list of accommodation, plus all the sights to see, places to visit and events on offer in Salzburg. You can book accommodation online.

In Salzburg, the tourist information offices are at the railway station and on Mozartplatz. You can get help in finding accommodation, obtain maps, book day trips and guided tours, and buy tickets.

The website of the Austrian National Tourist Office (ANTO, www.austria.info/uk) also has a wealth of information about Salzburg. Contacts overseas:

UK: toll free tel: 0800 400 200 00, info@austria.info.
US/Canada/Australia: info@austria.info.

TRANSPORT

Buses. Salzburg has a very efficient public transport system. You will find maps of the bus and trolley bus routes at the railway station and the bus information office on Mirabellplatz. It is possible to buy tickets from the driver as you board the bus and from the machines at some of the main bus stops, but it's cheaper to buy your tickets in advance. They are available from tobacconists (all marked with the Austria Tabak sign). You can buy blocks of five single tickets, 24-hour tickets or weekly tickets. Consider buying a Salzburg Card (see page 12), which includes free bus travel for the card's duration.

Post buses. These serve the outlying districts. Timetables can again be found at the railway station. You need to pay the driver when boarding the bus.

Lokalbahn. This commuter-train route serves many destinations to the north of the city, including Oberndorf and Maria Plain. Information is available at the railway station.

Taxis. Stands are scattered throughout the city. If you need to order a taxi, ask at your hotel reception or call 8111 for the taxi switchboard (www.taxi.at). Taxis run on a meter; fares start at €3.50 during the day and €4 in the evening.

VISAS AND ENTRY REQUIREMENTS

A valid passport is required to enter Austria. If you are a citizen of an EU country, the US, Canada, Australia or New Zealand, you do not require a visa.

All goods brought into Austria from EU countries must be duty-paid. Visitors coming from non-EU countries can bring in the following duty-free items: 200 cigarettes or 50 cigars or 250g of tobacco;

2 litres of alcohol (of less than 22 percent), and 1 litre of alcohol (of over 22 percent).

Austria is a member of Schengen, the EU countries that have signed a treaty to end internal border checkpoints and controls. This means that if you are arriving from another Schengen state (e.g. Germany, Italy) there are no more border controls. Police do, however, carry out spot checks on some routes near the borders.

Currency restrictions. There are no restrictions on the amount of foreign currency that can be brought into Austria.

VAT reimbursement. Non-EU citizens are entitled to reclaim VAT paid on goods over a certain value (*Mehrwehrtsteuer*). On purchase you must obtain a form from the sales assistant, get this stamped either at the airport or at the border when leaving the country and send it back to the shop. They will then transfer the amount to your bank account.

> I've nothing to declare. **Ich habe nichts zu verzollen.**
> It's for my personal use. **Das ist für meinen persönlichen Gebrauch.**

WEBSITES

A great deal of information about Salzburg can be obtained from the internet, some useful addresses are:

www.salzburg.info The Salzburg Tourist Office website

www.visit-salzburg.net Detailed information on sites, hotels and dining

www.stadt-salzburg.at Detailed website of the city's council, with an excellent section on Arts and Culture

www.weatheronline.co.uk/Austria/Salzburg.htm Reliable weather

data and long-range forecasts

www.salzburgfoundation.at Details of the Salzburg Arts Project, started in 2002, which initiated the creation of fascinating sculptures in the city

YOUTH HOSTELS

Salzburg has a good selection of cheap youth hostels. Probably the friendliest and most popular with backpackers is YoHo, Paracelsus Strasse 9, tel: 879 649, www.yoho.at. There is also the Jugend & Familiengästehaus (young persons' and family guesthouse) in Josef-Preis-Allee 18, tel: 57 083 613, www.jufa.at. For more information on youth hostels in Salzburg, see the Austrian Youth Hostel Association website: www.oejhw.or.at.

RECOMMENDED HOTELS

Thanks partly to the international reputation of its festivals, Salzburg has a fine selection of five- and four-star hotels. Three-star hotels tend to be less stylish – listed here are some of those that have their own charm and character. If you are on a tight budget, a *pension* (bed and breakfast) offers good value for money, and youth hostels provide basic, clean accommodation.

As Salzburg is not a huge city, even hotels slightly off the beaten track will be close enough to a bus route, and within easy reach of the city centre. Most listed below can help you organise tours and excursions around the city, while some are pick-up points on the tour routes.

You will be hard pushed to find a hotel that offers a large cooked breakfast, except the international ones. Elsewhere, breakfast is usually lighter, with bread, cereals, fruit, cold meats, cheese and yoghurt.

Prices are usually considerably higher in July and August, at Easter and for most of December. Some hotels take the opportunity to close during lulls between these peaks. Some smaller establishments, particularly *pensionen*, might not accept credit cards. Our price guide is for a double room in low season with breakfast:

€€€€€	over 220 euros
€€€€	160–220 euros
€€€	100–160 euros
€€	60–100 euros
€	below 60 euros

OLD TOWN

Altstadthotel Kasererbräu €€€ *Kaigasse 33, tel: 842 445, www.kaser erbraeu.at.* A charming, central hotel. The very different rooms have a homely feel about them. Some feature antique furniture, including solid, traditional wooden beds. Surprisingly for a small central hotel, it features a luxurious wellness facility that includes a sauna and a Turkish bath. 45 rooms.

Altstadthotel Weisse Taube €€€ *Kaigasse 9, tel: 842 404,* www.weisse taube.at. Managed by the Wollner family, this traditional hotel is in the pedestrianised part of the Old Town, right next to Mozartplatz. It was built in 1365, on land belonging to St Peter's Abbey. Although the rooms are not particularly of any era or theme, they are friendly and comfortable. Breakfast room and bar, but no restaurant. 31 rooms.

arthotel Blaue Gans €€€–€€€€ *Getreidegasse 41–43, tel: 842 491,* www. blauegans.at. The 'Blue Goose Art Hotel' calls itself a 'habitable work of art' and successfully fuses traditional and modern styles. The 37 rooms feature interesting works of art, crisp fabrics and warm lighting, all in a building that is nearly 700 years old.

Boutique Hotel am Dom €€€ *Goldgasse 17, tel: 842 765,* www.hotel amdom.at. In the heart of town, just minutes from the cathedral, this small hotel is an icon of contemporary design in Salzburg. Each of the 15 rooms has modern Italian-style furniture and is very creatively designed.

Hotel Elefant €€€–€€€€ *Sigmund-Haffner-Gasse 4, tel: 843 397,* www. elefant.at. Over 700 years old, and located very centrally in the Old Town, in an alleyway off the shopping street Getreidegasse. There is a curious story that King Max of Bavaria had an elephant, which stopped to look in the window of the building, since when it has been known as Elefant. The rooms have a pleasant contemporary decor, and you can dine in the *Ratsherrnkeller*, formerly a 17th-century wine cellar. 31 rooms.

Hotel Goldener Hirsch €€€€–€€€€€ *Getreidegasse 37, tel: 80840,* www. goldenerhirsch.com. With 65 rooms and 5 suites, this hotel has the feeling of an elegant private home. All the rooms are unique, with their own colour schemes and themes reminiscent of a 15th-century inn, combining antique furniture and modern amenities. Guests have a choice between the gourmet restaurant of chef Gernot Hicka and the cosy traditional restaurant *s'Herzl*, both specialising in Austrian cuisine.

Hotel Goldgasse €€€ Goldgasse 10, tel: 845 622, www.hotelgoldgasse. at. A very central location in the Old Town, based on one of Salzburg's oldest (14th-century) inns. Rooms are decorated in the style of traditional country homes, with antiques and art on the walls. The restaurant is a favourite haunt of the locals, which means it has good traditional cooking. 16 rooms.

Schloss Mönchstein €€€€€ *Mönchsberg Park 26, tel: 848 5550,* www.monchstein.at. Situated on top of the Mönchsberg and surrounded by a park, the hotel, with its exquisite restaurants, is one of the most spectacular five-star establishments in Austria. The individualistic bedrooms and bathrooms are out of this world. Needless to say, the location offers some of the best views of the city.

NEW TOWN

Altstadthotel Amadeus €€€ *Linzergasse 43–45, tel: 871 401,* www.hotel amadeus.at. Quaint and wholesome hotel in the centre of the New Town, in a 15th-century building that has been extensively renovated in a blend of tasteful modern elements and traditional comfort; some rooms have four-poster beds. The quietest rooms are at the rear, with views of the St Sebastian Cemetery. Breakfast is served in the spacious bistro-style café on the ground floor. 20 rooms.

Austrotel Salzburg am Mirabellplatz €€€ *Paris-Lodron-Strasse 1, tel: 881 688,* www.austrotel.at. Conveniently located next to the Mirabell Gardens. The five-storey building was once the residence of Prince Archbishop Paris Lodron. Despite its history, the hotel has all the modern facilities you will need. 70 rooms.

Gasthof Auerhahn €€ *Bahnhofstrasse 15, tel: 451 052,* www.auerhahn-salzburg.at. A family-run establishment with tasteful rooms, all 15 of which are decorated in a different style. The excellent restaurant has won gourmet awards for several years. The shady garden offers al fresco dining in summer. Located north of the railway station.

Hotel & Villa Auersperg €€–€€€ *Auerspergstrasse 61, tel: 889 440,* www.auersperg.at. Family-run hotel in two buildings with historic charm and contemporary chic. Tasteful leather sofas and wooden panelling in the public rooms; bedrooms have a warm, elegant feel. The hotel also has a roof terrace, an idyllic peaceful garden and a small spa. Bio breakfasts with great choice. 55 rooms.

Hotel Bristol €€€€€ *Makartplatz 4, tel: 873 557,* www.bristol-salzburg.at. Built around 1890, the Bristol is located between the Mirabell Gardens and Mozart's house. The rooms feature luxurious antique furnishings and thick-pile carpets. Expect sumptuous beds, chandeliers, and rich fabrics. Fine dining in the Polo Lounge restaurant, or unwind in the cosy Sketch Bar & Lounge. Close to the Paracelsus Kurhaus (spa & pool), where special rates apply to hotel guests. 60 rooms and suites.

Hotel Drei Kreuz €€ *Vogelweiderstrasse 9, tel: 872 790,* www.hoteldreikreuz.at. The name refers to the three crosses on the Kapuzinerberg. A modern, four-storey, family-run hotel featuring traditional rustic furniture and a lively bar. Breakfast room, but no restaurant. 24 rooms.

Hotel Hofwirt €€ *Schallmooser Hauptstrasse 1, tel: 872 1720,* www.hofwirt.net. A quiet, central hotel in a 100-year-old building at the top of the Linzergasse. The rooms (with noise-reducing windows), fully renovated in 2016, have a friendly, very modern feel. Airy breakfast room and stylish lobby bar. 87 rooms.

Hotel Mozart €€ *Franz-Josef-Strasse 27, tel: 872 274,* www.hotelmozart.at. Six-storey family-run hotel, five minutes' walk from Linzergasse and the Mirabell Gardens. Rooms are spacious – some large enough to sleep four comfortably – and cosy in a traditional, homely way. Friendly service. Breakfast only, no restaurant. 33 rooms.

Sacher Salzburg €€€€€ *Schwarzstrasse 5–7, tel: 88977,* www.sacher.com. Perhaps Salzburg's grandest hotel, founded in 1866 and the sister hotel to Sacher Vienna (famous for its Sachertorte chocolate cake). Located on the river with great views of the Old Town. The rooms range from standard to deluxe, though all are of five-star quality. The Sacher is large enough for a gym, sauna and steam bath, as well as a salon, a café and excellent restaurants serving both international cuisine and local specialities. If you look through the guest book, you will recognise many famous names. 111 rooms, including suites.

Stadtkrug €€€ *Linzergasse 20, tel: 873 5450*, www.stadtkrug.at. A popular base among performers at the Salzburg Festival, whose signed photographs adorn the walls. Rooms are sumptuously traditional with stone floors and ceiling beams. Good restaurant and roof garden with great views of the city. 40 rooms.

Star Inn Hotel Salzburg Gablerbräu €€€ *Richard-Mayer-Gasse 2, tel: 879 662,* www.starinnhotels.com/star-inn-hotel-premium-salzburg-gablerbraeu. This renovated brewery tavern, with some parts dating from the early 15th century, offers stylish family-friendly accommodation and modern comfort just a stone's throw from the river at the foot of Kapuzinerberg. 71 rooms.

Stein Hotel €€€ *Giselakai 3–5, tel: 874 3460,* www.hotelstein.at. Directly on the river Salzach, the four-star hotel has been in operation since 1399. At the top of the hotel is the famous Steinterrasse club/bar/lounge, with commanding views over the old city – the place to be for an afternoon tea or evening drinks.

Wolf-Dietrich €€€ *Wolf-Dietrich-Strasse 7, tel: 871 275,* www.salzburg-hotel.at. A homely, gay-friendly modern hotel in an old building in a quiet quarter, yet close to the New Town attractions. Very attentive service. Bio breakfast (organically sourced), complimentary afternoon tea and snacks. Lovely spa and indoor pool. Romantically themed rooms as well as suites. 40 rooms.

OUTSIDE THE CENTRE

Airport Hotel Salzburg €€€ *Dr-M-Laireiter-Strasse 9, tel: 850 020,* www.airporthotel.at. A modern hotel built in traditional Alpine style, with all the facilities of a four-star hotel, including a sauna, gym and indoor pool. Located right next to the airport (there are no flights at night) in the charming farming area of Wals. Rooms are functional but comfortable. Restaurant, coffee shop, bar-lounge, disco and casino. 32 rooms.

Astoria Hotel €€–€€€ *Maxglaner Hauptstrasse 7, tel: 834 277,* www.salz burgastoria.at. A 15-minute walk from the city centre, the Astoria is a tasteful and unpretentious modern place, privately owned and offering friendly service. Much of the decor features modern art. Some rooms have a winter garden balcony. No restaurant but a delightful coffee shop selling home-made cakes and other sweet treats. 30 rooms.

Doktorschössl €€ *Glaserstrasse 7 & 10, tel: 234 900,* www.doktor schloessl.com. A modern hotel with a picturesque house next door (housing the restaurant, breakfast room and bar), which received its name in 1670, when it was home to Dr Franz Mayr, physician to Prince Archbishop Wolf Dietrich von Raitenau and son-in-law of Santino Solari, the builder of Salzburg Cathedral. Most rooms have views of the Gaisberg or the Untersberg. Outdoor pool and pleasant garden.

Haus Am Moos € *Moosstrasse 186A, tel: 824 921,* www.ammoos. at. A stunning private house in the picturesque semi-rural area of Moosstrasse at the foot of the Untersberg. Close to the countryside and only a 15-minute bus ride into town. It is all about the Strasser family's personal touch. High-standard rooms, all with private bathroom, and a picture-perfect garden with large pool. Breakfast room only, no restaurant.

Haus Steiner € *Moosstrasse 156C, tel: 830 031,* www.haussteiner.com. A beautiful Alpine-style house surrounded by the countryside, but only a short bus ride from the centre of town. Family-run, traditional Austrian hospitality. Spacious rooms with fine views; some have balconies. Cheerful breakfast room (no restaurant).

Hotel Kobenzl-Vitalhotel €€€–€€€€ *Am Gaisberg 11, tel: 641 510,* www. kobenzl.at. Perched high above the city on the Gaisberg ('between Salzburg and the sky'), the Kobenzl has breathtaking views. The Panorama restaurant serves breakfast, lunch and dinner of the highest quality. But the main selling point is its health and beauty facilities: large indoor pool, saunas with steam shower, Turkish steam bath, infrared booths, and treatments ranging from Kneipp relaxation to 'colour acupuncture'. 40 rooms and suites, each with a balcony.

Pension Arenberg €€€ *Blumensteinstrasse 8, tel: 640 097*, www.arenberg-salzburg.at. On the slopes of the Kapuzinerberg, the hotel offers a quiet retreat from the city, with the personal touch of the Leopacher family, who pride themselves on traditional hosting. 13 spacious rooms, decorated in soft hues, all with balcony. Attractive garden, cheerful breakfast room (no restaurant).

Pension Elisabeth €€ *Vogelweiderstrasse 52, tel: 871 664*, www.pension-elisabeth.at. With some basic but very comfortable rooms and a charm of its own, this is a great place for budget travellers who still like a touch of elegance. A very bright, clean establishment. 24 rooms, some with shared facilities, and one apartment. Bicycles for rent.

Hotel Rosenvilla Salzburg €€€ *Höfelgasse 4, tel: 621 765*, www.rosenvilla.com. A pleasant hotel in the beautiful suburb of Aigen, east of the city, set in a small garden. A pond and a sun terrace. It feels as though you are in the country, but the town centre is only a 15-minute walk away. 15 stylish rooms and suites. No restaurant, breakfast only.

Villa Trapp €€€ *Traunstrasse 34, tel: 630 860*, www.villa-trapp.com. The former home of the real von Trapp family became a hotel in 2008 and is surrounded by Salzburg's largest private park. The villa was the residence of the von Trapps from 1923 to 1938. Now you can enjoy staying in the family's stylish rooms. 14 rooms, including suites. Breakfast only, no restaurant.

Villa Verde €€ *Leopoldskronstrasse 15, tel: 827 579*, www.villa-verde.at. Absolutely charming, small modern bed and breakfast in a quiet area near Schloss Leopoldskron (and the public swimming pool), with a good bus connection into the centre. All 11 rooms have en-suite bathrooms. Stylish breakfast room and idyllic gardens to relax in. Families are very welcome.

DICTIONARY

ENGLISH–GERMAN

adj adjective   **adv** adverb   **BE** British English   **n** noun   **prep** preposition   **v** verb

A

accept *v* akzeptieren

access *n* der Zutritt

accident der Unfall

accommodation die Unterkunft

account *n* (bank) das Konto

acupuncture die Akupunktur

adapter der Adapter

address *n* die Adresse

admission (price) der Eintritt

after nach; **~noon** der Nachmittag; **~shave** das Aftershave

age *n* das Alter

agency die Agentur

AIDS AIDS

air *n* die Luft; **~ conditioning** die Klimaanlage; **~-dry** lufttrocknen; **~ pump** die Luftpumpe; **~line** die Fluggesellschaft; **~mail** die Luftpost; **~plane** das Flugzeug; **~port** der Flughafen

aisle der Gang; **~ seat** der Platz am Gang

allergic allergisch; **~ reaction** die allergische Reaktion

allow erlauben

alone allein

alter *v* umändern

alternate route die Alternativroute

aluminum foil die Aluminiumfolie

amazing erstaunlich

ambulance der Krankenwagen

American *adj* amerikanisch

amusement park der Vergnügungspark

anemic anämisch

anesthesia die Anästhesie

animal das Tier

ankle das Fußgelenk

antibiotic *n* das Antibiotikum

antiques store das Antiquitätengeschäft

antiseptic cream die antiseptische Creme

apartment das Apartment

appendix (body part) der Blinddarm

appetizer die Vorspeise

appointment der Termin

arcade die Spielhalle

area code die Ortsvorwahl

arm *n* (body part) der Arm

aromatherapy die Aromatherapie

around (the corner) um; **~ (price)** ungefähr

arrival Ankunft

arrive ankommen

artery die Arterie

arthritis die Arthritis

art die Kunst

Asian *adj* asiatisch

aspirin das Aspirin

asthmatic asthmatisch

ATM der Bankautomat; **~ card** die Bankkarte

attack *v* angreifen

attraction (place) die Sehenswürdigkeit

attractive attraktiv

Australia das Australien

Australian *adj* australisch

automatic automatisch; **~ car** das Auto mit Automatikschaltung

available verfügbar

B

baby das Baby; **~ bottle** die Babyflasche; **~ wipe** das Baby-Pflegetuch; **~sitter** der Babysitter

back (body part) der Rücken; **~ache** die Rückenschmerzen; **~pack** der Rucksack

bag die Tasche

baggage [BE] das Gepäck; **~ claim** die Gepäckausgabe; **~ ticket** der Gepäckschein

bake *v* backen

bakery die Bäckerei

ballet das Ballett

bandage das Pflaster

bank *n* die Bank

bar (place) die Bar

barbecue (device) *n* der Grill

barber der Herrenfriseur

baseball der Baseball

basket (grocery store) der Einkaufskorb

basketball der Basketball

bathroom das Bad

battery die Batterie

battleground das Schlachtfeld

be *v* sein

beach der Strand

beautiful wunderschön; **~** schön

bed *n* das Bett; **~ and breakfast** die Pension

before vor

begin beginnen

beginner der Anfänger

behind (direction) hinter

beige *adj* beige
belt der Gürtel
best *adj* beste;
~ **before** mindestens
haltbar bis
better besser
bicycle das Fahrrad
big groß; ~**ger**
größerger
bike route die Radroute
bikini der Bikini
bill *n* **(money)** der
Geldschein; ~ *n* **(of
sale)** die Rechnung
bird der Vogel
birthday der Geburtstag
black *adj* schwarz
bladder die Blase
bland fad
blanket die Decke
bleed bluten
blender der Mixer
blood das Blut; ~ **pressure** der Blutdruck
blouse die Bluse
blue *adj* blau
board *v* einsteigen;
~**ing pass** die
Bordkarte
boat *n* das Boot
boil *v* kochen
bone *n* der Knochen
book *n* das Buch;
~**store** der Buchladen
boot *n* der Stiefel
boring langweilig
botanical garden der
botanische Garten
bother *v* belästigen
bottle *n* die Flasche;
~ **opener** der
Flaschenöffner
bowl *n* die Schüssel
boxing match der
Boxkampf

boy der Junge; ~**friend**
der Freund
bra der BH
bracelet das Armband
brake (car) die Bremse
breaded paniert
break *v* **(bone)** brechen
breakdown (car) die
Panne
breakfast *n* das
Frühstück
break-in (burglary) *n*
der Einbruch
breast die Brust; ~**feed**
v stillen
breathe atmen
bridge die Brücke
briefs (clothing) der
Schlüpfer
bring bringen
British *adj* britisch
broken kaputt;
~ **(bone)** gebrochen
brooch die Brosche
broom der Besen
brother der Bruder
brown *adj* braun
bug (insect) *n* das
Insekt
building das Gebäude
burn *v* brennen
bus *n* der Bus; ~ **station** der Busbahnhof;
~ **stop** die Bushal-
testelle; ~ **ticket** die
Busfahrkarte; ~ **tour**
die Busreise
business *adj*
Geschäfts-; ~ **card** die
Visitenkarte; ~ **center**
das Geschäftszentrum;
~ **class** die Business-
Class; ~ **hours** die
Öffnungszeiten
butcher *n* der Fleischer

buttocks der Po
buy *v* kaufen
bye auf Wiedersehen

C

cabaret das Kabarett
cable car die Seilbahn
cafe (place) das Café
call *v* **(phone)** anrufen;
~ *n* der Anruf ~ **col-
lect** ein R-Gespräch
führen
calorie die Kalorie
camera die Kamera;
~ **case** die Kamer-
atasche; **digital** ~ die
Digitalkamera
camp *v* campen;
~**ing stove** der
Campingkocher; ~**site**
der Campingplatz
can opener der
Dosenöffner
Canada das Kanada
Canadian *adj* kanadisch
cancel stornieren
candy die Süßigkeit
canned good die
Konserve
canyon der Canyon
car das Auto; ~ **hire
[BE]** die Autovermie-
tung; ~ **park [BE]** der
Parkplatz; ~ **rental**
die Autovermietung;
~ **seat** der Autositz
carafe die Karaffe
card *n* die Karte; **ATM** ~
die Bankkarte; **credit** ~
die Kreditkarte; **debit** ~
die EC-Karte; **phone** ~
die Telefonkarte
carry-on *n* **(piece of
hand luggage)** das
Handgepäckstück

cart (grocery store)
der Einkaufswagen;
~ **(luggage)** der
Gepäckwagen
carton (of cigarettes)
die Stange (Ziga-
retten); ~ **(of grocer-
ies)** die Packung
cash *n* das Bargeld;
~ *v* einlösen
cashier der Kassierer
casino das Casino
castle das Schloss
cathedral die
Kathedrale
cave *n* die Höhle
CD die CD
cell phone das Handy
Celsius Celsius
centimeter der
Zentimeter
certificate das
Zertifikat
chair *n* der Stuhl; ~ **lift**
der Sessellift
change *v* **(baby)**
wickeln; ~ **(buses)**
umsteigen;
~ **(money)** wechseln;
~ *n* **(money)** das
Wechselgeld
charge *v* **(credit card)**
belasten; ~ **(cost)**
verlangen
cheap billig; ~**er**
billiger
check *v* **(luggage)**
aufgeben; ~ **(on
something)** prüfen;
~ **(payment)** der
Scheck; ~**-in** das
Check-in; ~**ing ac-
count** das Girokonto;
~**-out** das Check-out
Cheers! Prost!

chemical toilet die Campingtoilette

chemist [BE] die Apotheke

chest (body part) die Brust; ~ pain der Brustschmerzen

chewing gum der Kaugummi

child das Kind; ~'s seat der Kinderstuhl

children's menu das Kindermenü

children's portion die Kinderportion

Chinese adj chinesisch

chopsticks die Stäbchen

church die Kirche

cigar die Zigarre

cigarette die Zigarette

class n die Klasse; business ~ die Business-Class; economy ~ die Economy-Class; first ~ die erste Klasse

classical music die klassische Musik

clean v reinigen; ~ adj (clothes) sauber; ~ing product das Reinigungsmittel

clear v (on an ATM) löschen

cliff die Klippe

cling film [BE] die Klarsichtfolie

close v (a shop) schließen

closed geschlossen

clothing die Bekleidung; ~ store das Bekleidungsgeschäft

club n der Club

coat der Mantel

coin die Münze

colander das Sieb

cold n (sickness) die Erkältung; ~ adj (temperature) kalt

colleague der Kollege

cologne das Kölnisch-wasser

color n die Farbe

comb n der Kamm

come v kommen

complaint die Beschwerde

computer der Computer

concert das Konzert; ~ hall die Konzerthalle

condition (medical) die Beschwerden

conditioner (hair) die Spülung

condom das Kondom

conference die Konferenz

confirm bestätigen

congestion (medical) der Blutstau

connect (internet) verbinden

connection (travel/internet) die Verbindung; ~ flight der Anschlussflug

constipated verstopft

consulate das Konsulat

consultant der Berater

contact v kontaktieren

contact lens die Kontaktlinse; ~ solution Kontaktlinsenlösung

contagious ansteckend

convention hall der Kongresssaal

conveyor belt das Förderband

cook v kochen

cool adj (temperature) kalt

copper n das Kupfer

corkscrew der Korkenzieher

cost v kosten

cotton die Baumwolle

cough v husten; ~ n der Husten

country code die Landesvorwahl

cover charge der Preis pro Gedeck

cream (ointment) die Creme

credit card die Kreditkarte

crew neck der runde Halsausschnitt

crib das Kinderbett

crystal n (glass) das Kristall

cup n die Tasse

currency die Währung; ~ exchange Währungsumtausch; ~ exchange office die Wechselstube

current account [BE] das Girokonto

customs der Zoll

cut v schneiden; ~ n (injury) der Schnitt

cute süß

cycling das Radfahren

D

damage v beschädigen

dance v tanzen; ~ club der Tanzclub; ~ing das Tanzen

dangerous gefährlich

dark adj dunkel

date n (calendar) das Datum

day der Tag

deaf adj taub

debit card die EC-Karte

deck chair der Liegestuhl

declare v (customs) deklarieren

decline v (credit card) ablehnen

deep adj tief

degree (temperature) das Grad

delay v verzögern

delete v (computer) löschen

delicatessen das Feinkostgeschäft

delicious lecker

denim das Denim

dentist der Zahnarzt

denture die Zahnpro-these

deodorant das Deodorant

department store das Kaufhaus

departure (plane) der Abflug

deposit v (money) einzahlen; ~ n (bank) die Einzahlung

desert n die Wüste

detergent das Waschmittel

develop v (film) entwickeln

diabetic adj diabetisch; n der Diabetiker

dial v wählen

diamond der Diamant

diaper die Windel

diarrhea der Durchfall

diesel der Diesel

difficult schwierig

digital digital;
~ **camera** die Digital-
kamera; ~ **photo** das
Digitalfoto; ~ **print**
der digitale Ausdruck

dining room das
Esszimmer

dinner das Abendessen

direction die Richtung

dirty schmutzig

disabled adj (person)
behindert; ~ **ac-
cessible** [BE]
behindertengerecht

disconnect (computer)
trennen

discount n der Rabatt;
die Ermäßigung

dishes (kitchen) das
Geschirr

dishwasher der
Geschirrspüler

dishwashing liquid
das Geschirrspülmittel

display n (device) das
Display; ~ **case** die
Vitrine

disposable n der
Einwegartikel; ~ **razor**
der Einweg-Rasierer

dive v tauchen

diving equipment
die Tauchausrüstung

divorce v sich scheiden
lassen

dizzy adj schwindelig

doctor n der Arzt

doll n die Puppe

dollar (U.S.) der
Dollar

domestic inländisch;
~ **flight** der
Inlandsflug

door die Tür

dormitory der
Schlafsaal

double bed das Dop-
pelbett

downtown n das
Stadtzentrum

dozen das Dutzend

drag lift der Schlepplift

dress (clothing) das
Kleid; ~ **code** die
Kleiderordnung

drink v trinken; ~ n
das Getränk; ~ **menu**
die Getränkekarte;
~**ing water** das
Trinkwasser

drive v fahren

**driver's license
number** die Führer-
scheinnummer

drop n (medicine) der
Tropfen

drowsiness die
Schläfrigkeit

dry clean chemisch
reinigen; ~**er's** die
chemische Reinigung

dubbed synchronisiert

during während

duty (tax) der Zoll;
~-**free** zollfrei

DVD die DVD

E

ear das Ohr; ~**ache** die
Ohrenschmerzen

earlier früher

early früh

earring der Ohrring

east n der Osten

easy leicht

eat v essen

economy class die
Economy-Class

elbow n der Ellenbogen

electric outlet die
Steckdose

elevator der Fahrstuhl

e-mail v eine E-Mail
senden; ~ n die
E-Mail; ~ **address** die
E-Mail-Adresse

emergency der Notfall;
~ **exit** der Notausgang

empty v entleeren

end v beenden; ~ n
das Ende

engaged (person)
verlobt

English adj englisch;
~ **(language)** das
Englisch

engrave eingravieren

enjoy genießen

enter v (place)
eintreten

entertainment die
Unterhaltung

entrance der Eingang

envelope der Umschlag

epileptic adj
epileptisch; ~n der
Epileptiker

equipment die
Ausrüstung

escalator die
Rolltreppe

e-ticket das E-Ticket

EU resident der
EU-Bürger

euro der Euro

evening n der Abend

excess baggage das
Übergepäck

exchange v um-
tauschen; ~ n (place)
die Wechselstube;
~ **rate** der Wech-
selkurs

excursion der Ausflug

excuse v entschuldigen

exhausted erschöpft

exit v verlassen; ~ n
der Ausgang

expensive teuer

experienced erfahren

expert der Experte

exposure (film) die
Belichtung

express adj Express-;
~ **bus** der Expressbus;
~ **train** der
Expresszug

extension (phone) die
Durchwahl

extra adj zusätzlich;
~ **large** extragroß

extract v (tooth) ziehen

eye das Auge

eyebrow wax die Au-
genbrauenkorrektur

F

face n das Gesicht

facial n die kosmet-
ische Gesichtsbe-
handlung

family n die Familie

fan n (appliance) der
Ventilator

far (distance) weit

farm der Bauernhof

far-sighted weitsichtig

fast adj schnell

fat free fettfrei

father der Vater

fax v faxen; ~ n das
Fax; ~ **number** die
Faxnummer

fee n die Gebühr

feed v füttern

ferry n die Fähre

fever n das Fieber

field (sports) der Platz

fill v (car) tanken

fill out v (form) ausfüllen

filling n (tooth) die Füllung

film n (camera) der Film

fine n (fee for breaking law) die Strafe

finger n der Finger; **~nail** der Fingernagel

fire n das Feuer; **~ department** die Feuerwehr; **~ door** die Feuertür

first adj erste; **~ class** erste Klasse

fit n (clothing) die Passform

fitting room die Umkleidekabine

fix v (repair) reparieren

fixed-price menu das Festpreismenü

flash photography das Fotografieren mit Blitzlicht

flashlight das Blitzlicht

flight n der Flug

flip-flops die Badelatschen

floor n (level) die Etage

florist der Florist

flower n die Blume

folk music die Volksmusik

food das Essen; **~ processor** die Küchenmaschine

foot n der Fuß

football game [BE] das Fußballspiel

for für

forecast n die Vorhersage

forest n der Wald

fork n die Gabel

form n (document) das Formular

formula (baby) die Babynahrung

fort die Festung

fountain n der Springbrunnen

freelance work die freiberufliche Arbeit

freezer der Gefrierschrank

fresh frisch

friend der Freund

frozen food die Tiefkühlkost

frying pan die Bratpfanne

full-time adj Vollzeit-

G

game n das Spiel

garage n (parking) die Garage; **~** n (for repairs) die Autowerkstatt

garbage bag der Abfallbeutel

gas (car) das Benzin; **~ station** die Tankstelle

gate (airport) das Gate

gay adj (homosexual) schwul; **~ bar** die Schwulenbar; **~ club** der Schwulenclub

gel n (hair) das Gel

generic drug das Generikum

German adj deutsch; **~** n (language) das Deutsch

Germany Deutschland

get off (a train/bus/ subway) aussteigen

gift n das Geschenk; **~ shop** der Geschenkwarenladen

girl das Mädchen; **~friend** die Freundin

give v geben

glass (drinking) das Glas; **~ (material)** das Glas

glasses die Brille

go v (somewhere) gehen

gold n das Gold

golf n das Golf; **~ course** der Golfplatz; **~ tournament** das Golfturnier

good adj gut; **~ afternoon** guten Tag; **~ day** guten Tag; **~ evening** guten Abend; **~ morning** guten Morgen; **~bye** auf Wiedersehen

gram das Gramm

grandchild das Enkelkind

grandparents die Großeltern

gray adj grau

green adj grün

grocery store das Lebensmittelgeschäft

ground floor das Erdgeschoss

groundcloth die Unterlegplane

group n die Gruppe

guide n (book) der Reiseführer; **~** n (person) der Fremdenführer; **~ dog** der Blindenhund

gym n (place) der Fitnessraum

gynecologist der Gynäkologe

H

hair das Haar; **~brush** die Haarbürste; **~cut** der Haarschnitt; **~ dryer** der Fön; **~ salon** der Friseursalon; **~spray** das Haarspray; **~style** die Frisur; **~ stylist** der Friseur

halal halal

half adj halb; **~** n die Hälfte; **~ hour** die halbe Stunde; **~-kilo** das halbe Kilo

hammer n der Hammer

hand n die Hand; **~ luggage** das Handgepäck; **~ wash** die Handwäsche; **~bag** [BE] die Handtasche

handicapped behindert; **~-accessible** behindertengerecht

hangover der Kater

happy glücklich

hat der Hut

have v haben; **~ sex** Sex haben

hay fever der Heuschnupfen

head (body part) n der Kopf; **~ache** die Kopfschmerzen; **~phones** die Kopfhörer

health die Gesundheit; **~ food store** das Reformhaus

hearing impaired hörgeschädigt

heart das Herz; **~ condition** die Herzkrankheit
heat v heizen; **~er** das Heizgerät; **~ing [BE]** die Heizung
hectare der Hektar
hello Hallo
helmet der Helm
help v helfen; **~** n die Hilfe
here hier
hi Hallo
high hoch; **~chair** der Kindersitz; **~lights (hair)** die Strähnchen; **~way** die Autobahn
hiking boots die Wanderschuhe
hill n der Berg
hire v **[BE] (a car)** mieten; **~ car [BE]** das Mietauto
hockey das Hockey
holiday [BE] der Urlaub
horsetrack die Pferderennbahn
hospital das Krankenhaus
hostel die Jugendherberge
hot (spicy) scharf; **~ (temperature)** heiß; **~ spring** heiße Quelle; **~ water** heißes Wasser
hotel das Hotel
hour die Stunde
house das Haus; **~hold goods** die Haushaltswaren; **~keeping services** der Hotelservice
how wie; **~ much** wie viel
hug v umarmen

hungry hungrig
hurt v wehtun
husband der Ehemann

I

ibuprofen das Ibuprofen
ice n das Eis; **~ hockey** das Eishockey
icy eisig
identification die Identifikation
ill krank
in in
include v beinhalten
indoor pool (public) das Hallenbad
inexpensive preisgünstig
infected infiziert
information (phone) die Auskunft; **~ desk** die Information
insect das Insekt; **~ bite** der Insektenstich; **~ repellent** der Insektenschutz
insert v **(card)** einführen
insomnia die Schlaflosigkeit
instant message das instant Message
insulin das Insulin
insurance die Versicherung; **~ card** die Versicherungskarte; **~ company** die Versicherungsgesellschaft
interesting interessant
intermediate fortgeschritten
international international; **~ flight** der internationale

Flug; **~ student card** der internationale Studentenausweis
internet das Internet; **~ cafe** das Internetcafé; **~ service** der Internetservice
interpreter der Dolmetscher
intersection die Kreuzung
intestine der Darm
introduce v **(person)** vorstellen
invoice n **[BE]** die Rechnung
Ireland das Irland
Irish adj irisch
iron v bügeln; **~** n **(clothes)** das Bügeleisen
Italian adj italienisch

J

jacket n die Jacke
Japanese adj japanisch
jar n **(for jam etc.)** das Glas
jaw n der Kiefer
jazz n der Jazz; **~ club** der Jazzclub
jeans die Jeans
jet ski die Jet-Ski
jeweler der Juwelier
jewelry der Schmuck
join v **(go with somebody)** mitkommen
joint n **(body part)** das Gelenk

K

key n der Schlüssel; **~ card** die Schlüsselkarte; **~ring** der Schlüsselring

kiddie pool das Kinderbecken
kidney (body part) die Niere
kilo das Kilo; **~gram** das Kilogramm; **~meter** der Kilometer
kiss v küssen
kitchen die Küche; **~ foil [BE]** die Aluminiumfolie
knee n das Knie
knife das Messer
kosher adj koscher

L

lace n **(fabric)** die Spitze
lactose intolerant laktoseintolerant
lake der See
large groß
last adj letzte
late (time) spät
launderette [BE] der Waschsalon
laundromat der Waschsalon
laundry (place) die Wäscherei **~ service** der Wäscheservice
lawyer n der Anwalt
leather n das Leder
leave v **(hotel)** abreisen; **~ (plane)** abfliegen
left adj, adv **(direction)** links
leg n das Bein
lens die Linse
less weniger
lesson n die Lektion; **take ~s** Unterricht nehmen
letter n der Brief

library die Bücherei

life jacket die Schwimmweste

lifeguard der Rettungsschwimmer

lift n [BE] der Fahrstuhl; ~ (ride) die Mitfahrgelegenheit; ~ pass der Liftpass

light n (cigarette) das Feuer; ~ n (overhead) die Lampe; ~bulb die Glühbirne

lighter n das Feuerzeug

like v mögen

line n (train/bus) die Linie

linen das Leinen

lip n die Lippe

liquor store das Spirituosengeschäft

liter der Liter

little wenig

live v leben; ~ music Livemusik

liver (body part) die Leber

loafers die Halbschuhe

local n (person) der Einheimische

lock v abschließen; ~ n das Schloss

locker das Schließfach

log off v (computer) abmelden

log on v (computer) anmelden

long adj lang; ~-sighted [BE] weitsichtig; ~-sleeved langärmlig

look v schauen; ~ for something etwas suchen

loose (fit) locker

lose v (something) verlieren

lost verloren; ~-and-found das Fundbüro

lotion die Lotion

louder lauter

love v (someone) lieben; ~ n die Liebe

low adj niedrig

luggage das Gepäck; ~ cart der Gepäckwagen; ~ locker das Gepäckschließfach; ~ ticket der Gepäckschein

lunch n das Mittagessen

lung die Lunge

luxury car das Luxusauto

M

machine washable maschinenwaschbar

magazine das Magazin

magnificent großartig

mail v mit der Post schicken; ~ n die Post; ~box der Briefkasten

main attraction die Hauptattraktion

main course das Hauptgericht

mall das Einkaufszentrum

man (adult male) der Mann

manager der Manager

manicure n die Maniküre

manual car das Auto mit Gangschaltung

map n die Karte; ~ n (town) der Stadtplan

market n der Markt

married verheiratet

marry heiraten

mass n (church service) die Messe

massage n die Massage

match n das Spiel

meal die Mahlzeit

measure v (someone) Maß nehmen

measuring cup der Messbecher

measuring spoon der Messlöffel

mechanic n der Mechaniker

medication (drugs) die Medikamente

medicine das Medikament

medium (steak) medium

meet v treffen

meeting n (business) das Meeting; ~ room das Konferenzzimmer

membership card der Mitgliedsausweis

memorial (place) das Denkmal

memory card die Speicherkarte

mend v (clothes) ausbessern

menstrual cramps die Menstruationskrämpfe

menu (restaurant) die Speisekarte

message die Nachricht

meter n (parking) die Parkuhr; ~ n (measure) der Meter

microwave n die Mikrowelle

midday [BE] der Mittag

midnight die Mitternacht

mileage die Meilenzahl

mini-bar die Mini-Bar

minute die Minute

missing (not there) weg

mistake n der Fehler

mobile home der Wohnwagen

mobile phone [BE] das Handy

mobility die Mobilität

monastery das Kloster

money das Geld

month der Monat

mop n der Wischmopp

moped das Moped

more mehr

morning n der Morgen

mosque die Moschee

mother n die Mutter

motion sickness die Reisekrankheit

motor n der Motor; ~ boat das Motorboot; ~cycle das Motorrad; ~way [BE] die Autobahn

mountain der Berg; ~ bike das Mountainbike

mousse (hair) der Schaumfestiger

mouth n der Mund

movie n der Film; ~ theater das Kino

mug v überfallen

multiple-trip ticket der Mehrfachfahrschein

muscle n der Muskel

museum das Museum

music die Musik; ~ store das Musikgeschäft

N

nail file die Nagelfeile
nail salon das Nagelstudio
name *n* der Name
napkin die Serviette
nappy [BE] die Windel
nationality die Nationalität
nature preserve das Naturreservat
nausea die Übelkeit
nauseous übel
near nahe; **~-sighted** kurzsichtig
nearby in der Nähe von
neck *n* der Nacken
necklace die Kette
need *v* brauchen
newspaper die Zeitung
newsstand der Zeitungskiosk
next *adj* nächste
nice schön
night die Nacht; **~club** der Nachtclub
no nein; **~ (not any)** kein
non-alcoholic nichtalkoholisch
non-smoking *adj* Nichtraucher
noon *n* der Mittag
north *n* der Norden
nose die Nase
note *n* [BE] (money) der Geldschein
nothing nichts
notify *v* benachrichtigen
novice der Anfänger
now jetzt
number *n* die Nummer
nurse *n* die Krankenschwester

O

office das Büro; **~ hours** die Bürozeiten
off-licence [BE] das Spirituosengeschäft
oil *n* das Öl
OK okay
old *adj* alt
on the corner an der Ecke
once (one time) einmal
one ein; (counting) eins; **~-day (ticket)** Tages-; **~-way ticket (airline)** das einfache Ticket, (bus/train/subway) die Einzelfahrkarte; **~-way street** die Einbahnstraße
only nur
open *v* öffnen; ~ *adj* offen
opera die Oper; **~ house** das Opernhaus
opposite *n* das Gegenteil
optician der Optiker
orange *adj* (color) orange
orchestra das Orchester
order *v* (restaurant) bestellen
outdoor pool das Freibad
outside *prep* draußen
over *prep* (direction) über; **~done** (meat) zu lang gebraten; **~heat** *v* (car) überhitzen; **~look** *n* (scenic place) der Aussichtsplatz; **~night**

über Nacht; **~-the-counter (medication)** rezeptfrei
oxygen treatment die Sauerstoffbehandlung

P

p.m. nachmittags
pacifier der Schnuller
pack *v* packen
package *n* das Paket
pad *n* [BE] die Monatsbinde
paddling pool [BE] das Kinderbecken
pain der Schmerz
pajamas der Pyjama
palace der Palast
pants die Hose
pantyhose die Strumpfhose
paper *n* (material) das Papier; **~ towel** das Papierhandtuch
paracetamol [BE] das Paracetamol
park *v* parken; ~ *n* der Park; **~ing garage** das Parkhaus; **~ing lot** der Parkplatz; **~ing meter** die Parkuhr
parliament building das Parlamentsgebäude
part (for car) das Teil; **~-time** *adj* Teilzeit-
pass through *v* (travel) durchreisen
passenger der Passagier
passport der Reisepass; **~ control** die Passkontrolle

password das Passwort
pastry shop die Konditorei
patch *v* (clothing) ausbessern
path der Pfad
pay *v* bezahlen; **~phone** das öffentliche Telefon
peak *n* (of a mountain) der Gipfel
pearl *n* die Perle
pedestrian *n* der Fußgänger
pediatrician der Kinderarzt
pedicure *n* die Pediküre
pen *n* der Stift
penicillin das Penicillin
penis der Penis
per *prep* ~ **day** pro Tag; **~ hour** pro Stunde; **~ night** pro Nacht; **~ week** pro Woche
perfume das Parfüm
period (menstrual) die Periode; ~ (of time) der Zeitraum
permit *v* erlauben
petrol [BE] das Benzin; **~ station** [BE] die Tankstelle
pewter das Zinn
pharmacy die Apotheke
phone *v* anrufen; ~ *n* das Telefon; **~ call** das Telefonat; **~ card** die Telefonkarte; **~ number** die Telefonnummer
photo das Foto; **~copy** die Fotokopie; **~graphy** die Fotografie
pick up *v* (person) abholen

picnic area der Rastplatz

piece n das Stück

Pill (birth control) die Pille

pillow n das Kissen

pink adj rosa

piste [BE] die Piste; **~ map [BE]** der Pistenplan

pizzeria die Pizzeria

place v (a bet) abgeben

plane n das Flugzeug

plastic wrap die Klarsichtfolie

plate n der Teller

platform [BE] (train) der Bahnsteig

platinum n das Platin

play v spielen; ~ n (theatre) das Stück; **~ground** der Spielplatz; **~pen** der Laufstall

please adv bitte

pleasure n die Freude

plunger die Saugglocke

plus size die Übergröße

pocket n die Tasche

poison n das Gift

poles (skiing) die Stöcke

police die Polizei; **~ report** der Polizeibericht; **~ station** das Polizeirevier

pond n der Teich

pool n der Pool

pop music die Popmusik

portion n die Portion

post n [BE] die Post; **~ office** die Post; **~box [BE]** der Briefkasten; **~card** die Postkarte

pot n der Topf

pottery die Töpferwaren

pound n (weight) das Pfund; **~ (British sterling)** das Pfund

pregnant schwanger

prescribe (medication) verschreiben

prescription das Rezept

press v (clothing) bügeln

price n der Preis

print v drucken; ~ n der Ausdruck

problem das Problem

produce n die Erzeugnis; **~ store** das Lebensmittelgeschäft

prohibit verbieten

pronounce aussprechen

Protestant der Protestant

public adj öffentlich

pull v ziehen

purple adj violett

purse n die Handtasche

push v drücken; **~chair [BE]** der Kinderwagen

Q

quality n die Qualität

question n die Frage

quiet adj leise

R

racetrack die Rennbahn

racket n (sports) der Schläger

railway station [BE] der Bahnhof

rain n der Regen; **~coat** die Regenjacke; **~forest** der Regenwald; **~y** regnerisch

rap n (music) der Rap

rape v vergewaltigen; **~ n** die Vergewaltigung

rare selten

rash n der Ausschlag

ravine die Schlucht

razor blade die Rasierklinge

reach v erreichen

ready bereit

real adj echt

receipt n die Quittung

receive v erhalten

reception (hotel) die Rezeption

recharge v aufladen

recommend empfehlen

recommendation die Empfehlung

recycling das Recycling

red adj rot

refrigerator der Kühlschrank

region die Region

registered mail das Einschreiben

regular n (fuel) das Normalbenzin

relationship die Beziehung

rent v mieten; **~ n** die Miete

rental car das Mietauto

repair v reparieren

repeat v wiederholen

reservation die Reservierung; **~ desk** der Reservierungsschalter

reserve v (hotel) reservieren

restaurant das Restaurant

restroom die Toilette

retired adj (from work) in Rente

return v (something) zurückgeben; ~ n [BE] (trip) die Hin- und Rückfahrt

reverse v (the charges) [BE] ein R-Gespräch führen

rib n (body part) die Rippe

right adj, adv (direction) rechts; **~ of way** die Vorfahrt

ring n der Ring

river n der Fluss

road map die Straßenkarte

rob v berauben

robbed beraubt

romantic adj romantisch

room n das Zimmer; **~ key** der Zimmerschlüssel; **~ service** der Zimmerservice

round trip die Hin- und Rückfahrt

route n die Route

rowboat das Ruderboot

rubbing alcohol der Franzbranntwein

rubbish n [BE] der Abfall; **~ bag [BE]** der Abfallbeutel

rugby das Rugby

ruin n die Ruine

rush n die Eile

S

sad traurig

safe adj (protected) sicher; **~ n (thing)** der Safe

sales tax die Mehrwertsteuer

same *adj* gleiche

sandals die Sandalen

sanitary napkin die Monatsbinde

sauna die Sauna

sauté *v* sautieren

save *v* (computer) speichern

savings (account) das Sparkonto

scanner der Scanner

scarf der Schal

schedule *v* planen; ~ *n* der Plan

school *n* die Schule

science die Wissenschaft

scissors die Schere

sea das Meer

seat *n* der Sitzplatz

security die Sicherheit

see *v* sehen

self-service *n* die Selbstbedienung

sell *v* verkaufen

seminar das Seminar

send *v* senden

senior citizen der Rentner

separated (person) getrennt lebend

serious ernst

service (in a restaurant) die Bedienung

sexually transmitted disease (STD) die sexuell übertragbare Krankheit

shampoo das Shampoo

sharp *adj* scharf

shaving cream die Rasiercreme

sheet *n* (bed) die Bettwäsche

ship *v* versenden

shirt das Hemd

shoe store das Schuhgeschäft

shoe der Schuh

shop *v* einkaufen; ~ *n* das Geschäft

shopping *n* das Einkaufen; ~ **area** das Einkaufszentrum; ~ **centre** [BE] das Einkaufszentrum; ~ **mall** das Einkaufszentrum

short kurz; **~-sleeved** kurzärmelig

shorts die kurze Hose

short-sighted [BE] kurzsichtig

shoulder *n* die Schulter

show *v* zeigen

shower *n* (bath) die Dusche

shrine der Schrein

sick *adj* krank

side *n* die Seite; ~ **dish** die Beilage; ~ **effect** die Nebenwirkung; ~ **order** die Beilage

sightseeing das Besichtigen von Sehenswürdigkeiten; ~ **tour** die Besichtigungstour

sign *v* (document) unterschreiben

silk die Seide

silver *n* das Silber

single *adj* (person) alleinstehend; ~ **bed** das Einzelbett; ~ **print** der Einzelabzug; ~ **room** das Einzelzimmer

sink *n* das Waschbecken

sister die Schwester

sit *v* sitzen

size *n* die Größe

ski *v* Ski fahren; ~ *n* der Ski; ~ **lift** der Skilift

skin *n* die Haut

skirt *n* der Rock

sleep *v* schlafen; **~er car** der Schlafwagen; **~ing bag** der Schlafsack; **~ing car** [BE] der Schlafwagen

slice *n* die Scheibe

slippers die Pantoffeln

slower langsamer

slowly langsam

small klein

smoke *v* rauchen

smoking (area) Raucher-

snack bar der Imbiss

sneakers die Turnschuhe

snowboard *n* das Snowboard

snowshoe *n* der Schneeschuh

snowy verschneit

soap *n* die Seife

soccer der Fußball

sock die Socke

some (with singular nouns) etwas; ~ (with plural nouns) einige

soother [BE] der Schnuller

sore throat die Halsschmerzen

south *n* der Süden

souvenir das Souvenir; ~ **store** das Souvenirgeschäft

spa das Wellness-Center

spatula der Spatel

speak *v* sprechen

specialist (doctor) der Spezialist

specimen die Probe

speeding die Geschwindigkeitsüberschreitung

spell *v* buchstabieren

spicy scharf; ~ (not bland) würzig

spine (body part) die Wirbelsäule

spoon *n* der Löffel

sports der Sport; ~ **massage** die Sportmassage

sprain *n* die Verstauchung

stadium das Stadion

stairs die Treppe

stamp *v* (ticket) entwerten; ~ *n* (postage) die Briefmarke

start *v* beginnen

starter [BE] die Vorspeise

station *n* (stop) die Haltestelle; **bus ~** der Busbahnhof; **gas ~** die Tankstelle; **petrol ~** [BE] die Tankstelle; **subway ~** die U-Bahn-Haltestelle; **train ~** der Bahnhof

statue die Statue

steakhouse das Steakhouse

steal *v* stehlen

steep *adj* steil

sterling silver das Sterlingsilber

sting *n* der Stich

stolen gestohlen

stomach der Magen; **~ache** die Bauchschmerzen

stool (bowel movement) der Stuhlgang
stop *v* **(bus)** anhalten; **~** *n* **(transportation)** die Haltestelle
store directory (mall) der Übersichtsplan
storey [BE] die Etage
stove *n* der Herd
straight *adv* **(direction)** geradeaus
strange seltsam
stream *n* der Strom
stroller (baby) der Kinderwagen
student (university) der Student; **~ (school)** der Schüler
study *n* studieren; **~ing** *n* das Studieren
stuffed gefüllt
stunning umwerfend
subtitle *n* der Untertitel
subway die U-Bahn; **~ station** die U-Bahn Haltestelle
suit *n* der Anzug; **~case** der Koffer
sun *n* die Sonne; **~block** das Sonnenschutzmittel; **~burn** der Sonnenbrand; **~glasses** die Sonnenbrille; **~ny** sonnig; **~screen** die Sonnencreme; **~stroke** der Sonnenstich
super *n* **(fuel)** das Superbenzin; **~market** der Supermarkt
surfboard das Surfboard
surgical spirit [BE] der Franzbranntwein

swallow *v* schlucken
sweater der Pullover
sweatshirt das Sweatshirt
sweet *n* **[BE]** die Süßigkeit; **~** *adj* **(taste)** süß
swelling die Schwellung
swim *n* schwimmen; **~suit** der Badeanzug
symbol (keyboard) das Zeichen
synagogue die Synagoge

T

table *n* der Tisch
tablet (medicine) die Tablette
take *v* nehmen
tampon *n* der Tampon
taste *v* **(test)** kosten
taxi *n* das Taxi
team *n* das Team
teaspoon der Teelöffel
telephone *n* das Telefon
temple (religious) der Tempel
temporary vorübergehend
tennis das Tennis
tent *n* das Zelt; **~ peg** der Zelthering; **~ pole** die Zeltstange
terminal *n* **(airport)** der Terminal
terrible schrecklich
text *v* **(send a message)** eine SMS schicken; **~** *n* der Text
thank *v* danken; **~ you** vielen Dank
the der?, das (neuter), die/
theater das Theater

theft der Diebstahl
there dort
thief der Dieb
thigh der Oberschenkel
thirsty durstig
this dieser?, dieses (neuter), diese/
throat der Hals
thunderstorm das Gewitter
ticket *n* die Fahrkarte; **~ office** der Fahrkartenschalter
tie *n* **(clothing)** die Krawatte
tight (fit) eng
tights [BE] die Strumpfhose
time die Zeit; **~table [BE] (transportation)** der Fahrplan
tire *n* der Reifen
tired müde
tissue das Gewebe
tobacconist der Tabakhändler
today *adv* heute
toe *n* der Zeh
toenail der Zehnagel
toilet [BE] die Toilette; **~ paper** das Toilettenpapier
tomorrow *adv* morgen
tongue *n* die Zunge
tonight heute Abend
to (direction) zu
tooth der Zahn
toothpaste die Zahnpasta
total *n* **(amount)** der Gesamtbetrag
tough *adj* **(food)** zäh
tour *n* die Tour
tourist der Tourist; **~ information office**

das Touristeninformationsbüro
tow truck der Abschleppwagen
towel *n* das Handtuch
tower *n* der Turm
town die Stadt; **~ hall** das Rathaus; **~ map** der Stadtplan; **~ square** der Rathausplatz
toy das Spielzeug; **~ store** der Spielzeugladen
track *n* **(train)** der Bahnsteig
traditional traditionell
traffic light die Ampel
trail *n* **(ski)** die Piste; **~ map** der Pistenplan
trailer (car) der Anhänger
train *n* der Zug; **~ station** der Bahnhof
transfer *v* **(change trains/flights)** umsteigen; **~ (money)** überweisen
translate übersetzen
trash *n* der Abfall
travel *n* das Reisen; **~ agency** das Reisebüro; **~ sickness** die Reisekrankheit; **~ers check [cheque BE]** der Reisescheck
tree der Baum
trim (hair) *v* nachschneiden
trip *n* die Reise
trolley [BE] (grocery store) der Einkaufswagen; **~ [BE] (luggage)** der Gepäckwagen

trousers [BE] die Hose
T-shirt das T-Shirt
tumble dry maschinentrocknen
turn off v (device) ausschalten
turn on v (device) anschalten
TV der Fernseher
tyre [BE] der Reifen

U

ugly hässlich
umbrella der Regenschirm
unbranded medication [BE] das Generikum
unconscious (faint) bewusstlos
underdone halb gar
underground n (BE) die U-Bahn; ~ **station [BE]** die U-Bahn-Haltestelle
underpants [BE] der Slip
understand v verstehen
underwear die Unterwäsche
United Kingdom (U.K.) das Großbritannien
United States (U.S.) die Vereinigten Staaten
university die Universität
unleaded (gas) bleifrei
upset stomach die Magenverstimmung
urgent dringend
urine der Urin
use v benutzen
username der

Benutzername
utensil das Haushaltsgerät

V

vacancy (room) das freie Zimmer
vacation der Urlaub
vaccination die Impfung
vacuum cleaner der Staubsauger
vaginal infection die vaginale Entzündung
valid gültig
valley das Tal
valuable adj wertvoll
value n der Wert
van der Kleintransporter
VAT [BE] die Mehrwertsteuer
vegan n der Veganer; ~ adj vegan
vegetarian n der Vegetarier; ~ adj vegetarisch
vehicle registration die Fahrzeugregistrierung
viewpoint (scenic) [BE] der Aussichtsplatz
village das Dorf
vineyard das Weingut
visa das Visum
visit v besuchen; ~**ing hours** die Besuchszeiten
visually impaired sehbehindert
vitamin das Vitamin

V-neck der V-Ausschnitt
volleyball game das Volleyballspiel
vomit v erbrechen; ~**ing** das Erbrechen

W

wait v warten; ~ n die Wartezeit
waiter der Kellner
waiting room der Warteraum
waitress die Kellnerin
wake v wecken; ~**-up call** der Weckruf
walk v spazieren gehen; ~ n der Spaziergang; ~**ing route** die Wanderroute
wallet die Geldbörse
war memorial das Kriegsdenkmal
warm v (something) erwärmen; ~ adj (temperature) warm
washing machine die Waschmaschine
watch v beobachten
waterfall der Wasserfall
wax v (hair) mit Wachs entfernen (Haare)
weather n das Wetter
week die Woche; ~**end** das Wochenende
weekly wöchentlich
welcome adj willkommen; **you're** ~ gern geschehen
west n der Westen
what was

wheelchair der Rollstuhl; ~ **ramp** die Rollstuhlrampe
when adv (at what time) wann
where wo
white adj weiß; ~ **gold** das Weißgold
who (question) wer
widowed verwitwet
wife die Ehefrau
window das Fenster; ~ **case** das Schaufenster
wine list die Weinkarte
wireless wireless; ~ **phone** das schnurlose Telefon
with mit
withdraw v (money) abheben; ~**al (bank)** die Abhebung
without ohne
woman die Frau
wool die Wolle
work v arbeiten
wrap v einpacken
wrist das Handgelenk
write v schreiben

Y

year das Jahr
yellow adj gelb
yes ja
yesterday adv gestern
young adj jung
youth hostel die Jugendherberge

Z

zoo der Zoo

GERMAN–ENGLISH

A

der Abend evening

das Abendessen dinner

der Abfall *n* trash [rubbish BE]

der Abfallbeutel garbage [rubbish BE] bag

abfliegen *v* leave (plane)

der Abflug departure (plane)

abgeben *v* place (a bet)

abheben *v* withdraw (money)

die Abhebung withdrawal (bank)

abholen *v* pick up (something)

ablehnen *v* decline (credit card)

abmelden *v* log off (computer)

der Abschleppwagen tow truck

abschließen *v* lock (door)

der Adapter adapter

die Adresse *n* address

das Aftershave aftershave

die Agentur agency

AIDS AIDS

die Akupunktur *n* acupuncture

akzeptieren *v* accept

allein alone; **~stehend** single (person)

allergisch allergic; **die allergische Reaktion** allergic reaction

alt *adj* old

das Alter *n* age

die Alternativroute alternate route

die Aluminiumfolie aluminum [kitchen BE] foil

amerikanisch American

die Ampel traffic light

anämisch anemic

die Anästhesie anesthesia

der Anfänger beginner/novice

angreifen *v* attack

anhalten *v* stop

der Anhänger trailer

ankommen arrive

die Ankunft arrival

anmelden *v* log on (computer)

der Anruf *n* call

anrufen *v* call

anschalten *v* turn on (device)

ansteckend contagious

das Antibiotikum *n* antibiotic

das Antiquitätengeschäft antiques store

antiseptisch antiseptic

der Anwalt lawyer

die Anzahlung deposit (car rental)

der Anzug *n* suit

das Apartment apartment

die Apotheke pharmacy [chemist BE]

arbeiten *v* work

arbeitslos *adj* unemployed

der Arm *n* arm (body part)

die Aromatherapie aromatherapy

die Arterie artery

die Arthritis arthritis

der Arzt doctor

asiatisch Asian

das Aspirin aspirin

asthmatisch asthmatic

atmen breathe (place)

attraktiv attractive

auf Wiedersehen goodbye

aufladen *v* recharge

das Auge eye

ausbessern *v* mend (clothing)

der Ausfluss discharge (bodily fluid)

ausfüllen *v* fill out (form)

der Ausgang *n* exit

ausgeschlafen well-rested

die Auskunft information (phone)

die Ausrüstung equipment

ausschalten turn off (device)

der Ausschlag rash

der Aussichtsplatz viewpoint [BE]

aussprechen pronounce

aussteigen get off (a train/bus/subway)

Australien Australia

der Australier Australian

das Auto car; **~ mit Automatikschaltung** automatic car; **~ mit Gangschaltung** manual car

die Autobahn highway [motorway BE]

automatisch automatic

der Autositz car seat

die Autovermietung car rental [hire BE]

B

das Baby baby

die Babyflasche baby bottle

die Babynahrung formula (baby)

das Baby-Pflegetuch baby wipe

der Babysitter babysitter

backen bake

die Bäckerei bakery

das Bad bathroom

der Badeanzug swimsuit

die Badelatschen flip-flops

der Bahnhof train [railway BE] station

der Bahnsteig track [platform BE]

das Ballett ballet

die Bank bank (money)

der Bankautomat ATM

die Bankkarte ATM card

die Bar bar (place)

das Bargeld *n* cash
der Baseball baseball (game)
der Basketball basketball (game)
die Batterie battery
die Bauchschmerzen stomachache
der Bauernhof *n* farm
der Baum tree
die Baumwolle cotton
die Beaufsichtigung supervision
die Bedienung service (in a restaurant)
beenden *v* exit (computer)
beginnen begin
behindert handicapped; **~engerecht** handicapped [disabled BE]-accessible
beige *adj* beige
die Beilage side order
das Bein leg
beinhalten include (tax)
die Bekleidung clothing
das Bekleidungsgeschäft clothing store
belasten *v* charge (credit card)
belästigen bother
die Belichtung exposure (film)
benachrichtigen notify
benutzen *v* use
der Benutzername username
das Benzin gas [petrol BE]
beobachten *v* watch
der Berater consultant
berauben rob

beraubt robbed
bereit ready
der Berg hill; **~** mountain
beschädigen *v* damage
beschädigt damaged
die Beschwerde complaint
die Beschwerden condition (medical)
der Besen broom
die Besichtigungstour sightseeing tour
besser better
bestätigen confirm
beste *adj* best
bestellen *v* order (restaurant)
besuchen *v* visit
die Besuchszeiten visiting hours
das Bett *n* bed
die Bettwäsche sheets
bewusstlos unconscious (condition)
bezahlen pay
die Beziehung relationship
der BH bra
der Bikini bikini
billig cheap
billiger cheaper
bitte please
die Blase bladder
blau *adj* blue
bleifrei unleaded (gas)
der Blinddarm appendix (body part)
der Blindenhund guide dog
das Blitzlicht flashlight
die Blume *n* flower
die Bluse blouse
das Blut blood

der Blutdruck blood pressure
bluten bleed
der Blutstau congestion
das Boot boat
die Bordkarte boarding pass
der botanische Garten botanical garden
der Boxkampf boxing match
die Bratpfanne frying pan
brauchen *v* need
braun *adj* brown
brechen *v* break
die Bremse brakes (car)
brennen *v* burn
der Brief letter
der Briefkasten mailbox [postbox BE]
die Briefmarke *n* stamp (postage)
die Brille glasses (optical)
bringen bring
britisch British
die Brosche brooch
die Brücke bridge
der Bruder brother
die Brust breast; **~** chest **~schmerzen** chest pain
das Buch *n* book
die Bücherei library
der Buchladen bookstore
buchstabieren *v* spell
das Bügeleisen *v* iron (clothes)
bügeln *v* iron
das Büro office
die Bürozeiten office hours

der Bus bus; **~bahnhof** bus station; **~fahrschein** bus ticket
die Bushaltestelle bus stop
die Business-Class business class
die Bustour bus tour

C

das Café cafe (place)
campen *v* camp
der Campingkocher camping stove
der Campingplatz campsite
die Campingtoilette chemical toilet
der Canyon canyon
das Casino casino
die CD CD
Celsius Celsius
das Check-in check-in
das Check-out check-out
chinesisch Chinese
der Club *n* club
der Computer computer
die Creme *n* cream (ointment)

D

danken thank
der Darm intestine
das (neuter) the
das Datum *n* date (calendar)
die Decke blanket
das Denkmal memorial (place)
das Deodorant deodorant
der the
das Deutsch German; **~land** Germany

der Diabetiker *n* diabetic

der Diamant diamond

die the

der Dieb thief; **~stahl** theft

diese this

der Diesel diesel

dieser this

dieses (neuter) this

digital digital

der Digitaldruck digital print

das Digitalfoto digital photo

die Digitalkamera digital camera

das Display *n* display

Dollar dollar (U.S.)

der Dolmetscher interpreter

das Doppelbett double bed

das Dorf village

dort there

der Dosenöffner can opener

draußen outside

dringend urgent

drucken *v* print

drücken *v* push

dunkel *adj* dark

der Durchfall diarrhea

durchreisen pass through

durstig thirsty

die Dusche *n* shower

das Dutzend dozen

die DVD DVD

E

echt real

die EC-Karte debit card

die Ecke *n* corner; **an der Ecke** on the corner

die Economy-Class economy class

die Ehefrau wife

der Ehemann husband

die Eile *n* rush

die Einbahnstraße one-way street

einbrechen *v* break in (burglary)

einchecken *v* check in

einführen *v* insert

der Eingang entrance

eingravieren engrave

der Einheimische *n* local (person)

einkaufen *v* shop

das Einkaufen shopping

der Einkaufskorb basket (grocery store)

der Einkaufswagen cart [trolley BE] (grocery store)

das Einkaufszentrum shopping mall [centre BE]; **~** shopping area (town)

einlösen *v* cash (check)

einmal once

einpacken *v* wrap (parcel)

eins one

das Einschreiben registered mail

einsteigen *v* board (bus)

eintreten *v* enter

der Eintritt admission (fee)

der Einwegartikel *n* disposable

der Einweg-Rasierer disposable razor

einzahlen *v* deposit (money)

die Einzahlung *n* deposit (bank)

der Einzelabzug single print

das Einzelbett single bed

das Einzelzimmer single room

das Eis *n* ice; **~hockey** ice hockey

der Ellenbogen elbow

die E-Mail *n* e-mail; **~-Adresse** e-mail address; **~ senden** *v* e-mail

empfehlen recommend

die Empfehlung recommendation

eng tight (fit)

englisch English

der Enkel grandchild

entleeren *v* empty

entschuldigen *v* excuse

entwerten *v* stamp (ticket)

entwickeln *v* develop (film)

epileptisch *adj* epileptic

erbrechen *v* vomit

erfahren *adj* experienced

erhalten receive

die Erkältung *n* cold (sickness)

erklären *v* explain

erlauben *v* allow

ernst serious

erreichen *v* reach

erschöpft exhausted

erstaunlich amazing

erste Klasse first class

erste *adj* first

erwärmen *v* warm (something)

essen eat

das Essen food

das Esszimmer dining room

die Etage floor [storey BE]

das E-Ticket e-ticket

etwas something; **~ mehr...** some more...

der EU-Bürger EU resident

der Euro euro

die Exkursion excursion

der Experte *n* expert

der Express *n* express; **~bus** express bus

extra extra; **~ groß** extra large

F

die Fähre ferry

fahren *v* drive

die Fahrkarte ticket

der Fahrkartenschalter ticket office

das Fahrrad *n* bicycle

der Fahrradweg bike route

der Fahrstuhl elevator [lift BE]

die Fahrzeugregistrierung vehicle registration

die Familie family

die Farbe *n* color

das Fax *n* fax

faxen *v* fax

die Faxnummer fax number

der Fehler *n* mistake

fehlen be missing

der Urlaub vacation [holiday BE]

das Feinkostgeschäft delicatessen

das Fenster window

der Fernseher television

das Festpreismenü fixed-price menu

die Festung fort

fettfrei fat free

das Feuer n fire

die Feuertür fire door

die Feuerwehr fire department

das Feuerzeug lighter

das Fieber fever

filetiert fileted (food)

der Film film (camera); ~ movie (cinema)

der Finger n finger

der Fingernagel fingernail

der Fitnessraum gym (workout)

die Flasche n bottle

der Flaschenöffner bottle opener

der Fleischer butcher

der Florist florist

der Flug flight

die Fluggesellschaft airline

der Flughafen airport

das Flugzeug airplane

der Fluss river

der Fön hair dryer

das Förderband conveyor belt

das Formular n form

fortgeschritten intermediate

das Foto photo

die Fotografie photography

fotografieren take a photo

die Fotokopie photocopy

die Frage n question

der Franzbranntwein rubbing alcohol [surgical spirit BE]

die Frau woman

freiberufliche Arbeit freelance work

frei adj free

das Fremdenverkehrsbüro tourist information office

die Freude pleasure

der Freund boyfriend; friend

die Freundin girlfriend; friend

frisch fresh

die Frischhaltefolie plastic wrap

der Friseur barber, hairstylist

der Friseursalon hair salon

die Frisur hairstyle

früh early

das Frühstück breakfast

der Führer guide

die Führerscheinnummer driver's license number

das Fundbüro lost-and-found

für for

der Fuß foot; ~ball soccer

das Fußballspiel soccer match [football game BE]

der Fußgänger n pedestrian

das Fußgelenk n ankle

füttern v feed

G

die Gabel fork

der Gang aisle

die Garage garage

das Gate gate (airport)

das Gebäude building

geben v give

die Gebühr fee

der Geburtstag birthday

gefährlich dangerous

der Gefrierschrank freezer

das Gegenteil n opposite

gehen v go (somewhere)

gekocht stewed

das Gel gel (hair)

gelb adj yellow

das Gelbgold yellow gold

das Geld money

die Geldbörse wallet

der Geldschein n bill [note BE] (money)

das Gelenk joint (body part)

das Generikum generic drug [unbranded medication BE]

genießen v enjoy

das Gepäck baggage [luggage BE]

die Gepäckausgabe baggage claim

der Gepäckschein baggage [luggage BE] ticket

das Gepäckschließfach baggage [luggage BE] locker

der Gepäckwagen baggage [luggage BE] cart

geradeaus straight

gern geschehen you're welcome

das Geschäft business; ~ store ~sverzeichnis store directory; ~szentrum business center

das Geschenk gift

der Geschenkwarenladen gift shop

das Geschirr dishes (kitchen)

der Geschirrspüler dishwasher

das Geschirrspülmittel dishwashing liquid

geschlossen closed

die Geschwindigkeitsüber-schreitung speeding

das Gesicht n face

gestern yesterday

gestohlen stolen

die Gesundheit health

das Getränk n drink

die Getränkekarte drink menu

getrennt lebend separated (person)

das Gewitter thunderstorm

gewürfelt diced (food)

das Gift n poison

der Gipfel peak (of a mountain)

das Girokonto checking [current BE] account

das Glas glass

gleich same

glücklich happy

die Glühbirne lightbulb
golden golden
der Golfplatz golf course
das Golfturnier golf tournament
das Grad degree (temperature)
das Gramm gram
grau *adj* gray
der Grill *n* barbecue
groß big; **~ large**
großartig magnificent
das Großbritannien United Kingdom (U.K.)
die Größe *n* size
die Großeltern grandparents
größer bigger; **~ larger**
grün *adj* green
die Gruppe *n* group
gültig valid
der Gürtel belt
gut *adj* good; *adv* well; **~enAbend** good evening; **~en Morgen** good morning; **~en Tag** good day
der Gynäkologe gynecologist

H

das Haar hair
die Haarbürste hairbrush
der Harfestiger mousse (hair)
der Haarschnitt haircut
das Haarspray hairspray
haben *v* have
halal halal
halb half; **~gar** underdone; **die ~e Stunde** half hour; **das ~e Kilo** half-kilo

die Halbschuhe loafers
halbtags part-time
das Hallenbad indoor pool
Hallo hello
der Hals throat
die Halsschmerzen sore throat
die Haltestelle *n* stop
der Hammer *n* hammer
die Hand *n* hand
das Handgelenk wrist
das Handgepäck hand luggage
die Handtasche purse [handbag BE]
das Handtuch towel
Handwäsche hand wash
das Handy cell [mobile BE] phone
hässlich ugly
die Hauptattraktion main attraction
das Hauptgericht main course
das Haus *n* house
das Haushaltsgerät utensil
die Haushaltswaren household goods
die Haut *n* skin
heiraten *v* marry
heiß hot (temperature); **~eQuelle** hot spring; **~esWasser** hot water
heizen *v* heat
die Heizung heating
der Hektar hectare
helfen *v* help
der Helm helmet
das Hemd shirt
der Herd stove
das Herz heart

die Herzkrankheit heart condition
der Heuschnupfen hay fever
heute today; **~ Abend** tonight
hier here
die Hilfe *n* help
die Hin- und Rückfahrt round-trip
Hinfahrt- one-way (ticket)
hinter behind (direction)
hoch high
das Hockey hockey
die Höhle *n* cave
hörgeschädigt hearing impaired
die Hose pants [trousers BE]
das Hotel hotel
hungrig hungry
husten *v* cough
der Husten *n* cough
der Hut hat

I

das Ibuprofen ibuprofen
die Identifikation identification
die Impfung vaccination
in in
infiziert infected
die Information information; **~ information desk**
inländisch domestic
der Inlandsflug domestic flight
das Insekt bug
der Insektenschutz insect repellent
der Insektenstich insect bite

die Instant Message instant message
das Insulin insulin
interessant interesting
international international; **der ~e Studentenausweis** international student card; **der ~e Flug** international flight
das Internet internet; **~café** internet cafe
der Internet-service internet service
irisch *adj* Irish
Irland Ireland
italienisch *adj* Italian

J

ja yes
die Jacke jacket
das Jahr year
japanisch Japanese
der Jazz jazz; **~club** jazz club
die Jeans jeans
der Jeansstoff denim
der Jet-ski jet ski
jetzt now
die Jugendherberge hostel; **~ youth hostel**
jung *adj* young
der Junge boy
der Juwelier jeweler

K

das Kabarett cabaret
das Kaffeehaus coffee house
die Kalorie calorie
kalt *adj* cold (temperature); **~ cool** (temperature)
die Kamera camera

die Kameratasche camera case
der Kamm *n* comb
das Kanada Canada
kanadisch *adj* Canadian
die Karaffe carafe
die Karte *n* card;
~ map
der Kassierer cashier
der Kater hangover (alcohol)
die Kathedrale cathedral
kaufen *v* buy
das Kaufhaus department store
der Kaugummi chewing gum
der Kellner waiter
die Kellnerin waitress
die Kette necklace
der Kiefer jaw
das Kilo kilo; **~gramm** kilogram
der Kilometer kilometer
das Kind child
der Kinderarzt pediatrician
das Kinderbecken kiddie pool
das Kinderbett cot
die Kinderkarte children's menu
die Kinderportion children's portion
der Kindersitz highchair
der Kinderstuhl child's seat
der Kinderwagen stroller
das Kino movie theater
die Kirche church
das Kissen pillow

die Klarsichtfolie plastic wrap [cling film BE]
die Klasse class
die klassische Musik classical music
das Kleid *n* dress (clothing)
die Kleiderordnung dress code
klein small
der Kleintransporter van
die Klimaanlage air conditioning
die Klippe cliff
das Kloster monastery
das Knie *n* knee
der Knochen *n* bone
kochen *v* boil; ~ cook
das Kölnischwasser cologne
der Koffer suitcase
der Kollege colleague
kommen *v* come
die Konditorei pastry shop
das Kondom condom
die Konferenz conference
das Konferenzzimmer meeting room
der Kongressaal convention hall
die Konserve canned good
das Konsulat consulate
kontaktieren *v* contact
die Kontaktlinse contact lens
die Kontaktlinsenlösung contact lens solution
das Konto *n* account

das Konzert concert
die Konzerthalle concert hall
der Kopf *n* head (body part)
die Kopfhörer headphones
die Kopfschmerzen headache
der Korkenzieher corkscrew
koscher kosher
kosmetisch *adj* cosmetic; **~e Gesichtsbehandlung** facial (treatment)
kosten *v* cost; ~ taste
krank ill; ~ sick
das Krankenhaus hospital
die Krankenschwester *n* nurse
der Krankenwagen ambulance
die Krawatte tie (clothing)
die Kreditkarte credit card
die Kreuzung intersection
das Kriegsdenkmal war memorial
das Kristall crystal (glass)
die Küche kitchen
die Küchenmaschine food processor
der Kühlschrank refrigerator
die Kunst art
das Kupfer copper
kurz short; **~e Hose** shorts
kurzärmelig short-sleeved

kurzsichtig near- [short- BE] sighted
küssen *v* kiss

L

laktoseintolerant lactose intolerant
die Lampe *n* light (overhead)
die Landesvorwahl country code
landwirtschaftliches Erzeugnis produce
lang *adj* long; **~ärmlig** long-sleeved;
langsam slow; **~er** slower
langweilig boring
der Laufstall playpen
lauter louder
leben *v* live
das Lebensmittelgeschäft grocery store
die Leber liver (body part)
lecker delicious
das Leder leather
leicht easy
das Leinen linen
leise quiet
die Lektion lesson
letzte *adj* last
die Liebe *n* love
lieben *v* love (someone)
der Liegestuhl deck chair (ferry)
der Liftpass lift pass
die Linie line (train)
links left (direction)
die Linse lens
die Lippe lip
der Liter liter
Livemusik live music
locker loose (fit)
der Löffel *n* spoon

löschen v clear (on an ATM); ~ v delete (computer)
die Lotion lotion
die Luftpost n airmail
die Luftpumpe air pump
lufttrocknen v air dry
die Lunge lung

M

das Mädchen girl
das Magazin magazine
der Magen stomach
die Magenverstimmung upset stomach
die Mahlzeit meal
der Manager manager
die Maniküre n manicure
der Mann man (male)
der Mantel n coat
der Markt market
maschinentrocknen tumble dry
die Massage n massage
mechanisch adj mechanic
das Medikament medicine
die Medikamente medication
medium adj medium (meat)
das Meer sea
mehr more
die Mehrwertsteuer sales tax [VAT BE]
die Menstruationskrämpfe menstrual cramps
die Messe mass (church service)

messen v measure (someone)
das Messer knife
der Messbecher measuring cup
der Messlöffel measuring spoon
das Mietauto rental [hire BE] car
mieten v rent [hire BE]
die Mikrowelle n microwave
mild mild
die Mini-Bar mini-bar
die Minute minute
mit with; ~ **Bedienung** full-service
die Mitgliedskarte membership card
mitkommen v join
mitnehmen give somebody a lift (ride)
Mittag noon [midday BE]
das Mittagessen n lunch
Mitternacht midnight
der Mixer blender
die Mobilität mobility
mögen v like
der Monat month
die Monatsbinde sanitary napkin [pad BE]
der Mopp n mop
das Moped moped
morgen tomorrow
der Morgen morning
die Moschee mosque
der Moslem Muslim
das Motorboot motor boat
das Motorrad motorcycle
das Mountainbike mountain bike

müde tired
der Mund mouth
die Münze coin
das Münztelefon pay phone
das Museum museum
die Musik music
das Musikgeschäft music store
der Muskel muscle
die Mutter mother

N

nach after
der Nachmittag afternoon
nachprüfen v check (on something)
die Nachricht message
nachschneiden trim (haircut)
nächste adj next
die Nacht night
der Nachtclub nightclub
der Nacken neck
die Nagelfeile nail file
das Nagelstudio nail salon
nahe prep near
die Nähe vicinity; **in der Nähe** nearby
der Name n name
die Nase nose
die Nationalität nationality
das Naturreservat nature preserve
die Nebenstelle extension (phone)
die Nebenwirkung side effect
nehmen v take
nein no

Nichtraucher- non-smoking (area)
nichts nothing
niedrig low
die Niere kidney (body part)
der Norden n north
normal regular
der Notausgang emergency exit
der Notfall emergency
die Nummer n number
nur only; ~ **just**

O

obere adj upper
der Oberschenkel thigh
offen adj open
öffentlich adj public
öffnen v open
die Öffnungszeiten business hours
ohne without
das Ohr ear
die Ohrenschmerzen earache
der Ohrring earring
OK okay
das Öl n oil
die Oper opera
das Opernhaus opera house
der Optiker optician
orange adj orange (color)
das Orchester orchestra
die Ortsvorwahl area code
der Osten n east

P

packen v pack
die Packung carton; ~ packet

das Paket package
der Palast palace
paniert breaded
die Panne breakdown (car)
die Pantoffeln slippers
das Papier n paper
das Papierhandtuch paper towel
das Paracetamol acetaminophen [paracetamol BE]
das Parfüm n perfume
der Park n park
parken v park
das Parkhaus parking garage
der Parkplatz parking lot [car park BE]
die Parkuhr parking meter
das Parlamentsgebäude parliament building
das Parterre ground floor
der Passagier passenger
die Passform fit (clothing)
die Passkontrolle passport control
das Passwort password
die Pediküre pedicure
das Penicillin penicillin
der Penis penis
die Pension bed and breakfast
die Periode period (menstrual)
die Perle pearl
der Pfad path
die Pferderennbahn horsetrack

das Pflaster bandage
das Pfund n pound (weight)
das Pfund pound (British sterling)
die Pille Pill (birth control)
die Piste n trail [piste BE]
der Pistenplan trail [piste BE] map
die Pizzeria pizzeria
der Plan n schedule [timetable BE]; ~ map
planen v plan
das Platin platinum
die Platte flat tire
der Platz field (sports); ~ seat; ~ am Gang aisle seat
die Plombe filling (tooth)
der Po buttocks
die Polizei police
der Polizeibericht police report
das Polizeirevier police station
der Pool n pool
die Popmusik pop music
die Portion n portion
die Post mail [post BE]; ~ post office
die Postkarte postcard
der Preis price; ~ pro Gedeck cover charge
preisgünstig inexpensive
pro per; ~ Nacht per night; ~ Stunde per hour; ~ Tag per day; ~ Woche per week
das Problem problem
Prost! Cheers!

die Prothese denture
die Puppe doll
der Pyjama pajamas

Q

die Qualität n quality
die Quittung receipt

R

das R-Gespräch collect call [reverse charge call BE]
ein R-Gespräch führen v call collect [to reverse the charges BE]
der Rabatt discount
das Radfahren cycling
der Rap rap (music)
die Rasiercreme shaving cream
die Rasierklinge razor blade
der Rastplatz picnic area
das Rathaus town hall
der Rathausplatz town square
rauchen v smoke
Raucher- smoking (area)
die Rechnung bill [invoice BE] (of sale)
rechts right (direction)
das Recycling recycling
das Reformhaus health food store
der Regen n rain
die Regenjacke raincoat
der Regenschirm umbrella
der Regenwald rainforest

die Region region
regnerisch rainy
der Reifen tire [tyre BE]
reinigen v clean; **chemisch ~** dry clean
die Reinigung dry cleaner's
die Reinigungsmittel cleaning supplies
die Reise trip; ~ journey
das Reisebüro travel agency
der Reiseführer guide book
die Reisekrankheit motion sickness
der Reisepass passport
der Reisescheck traveler's check [cheque BE]
die Rennbahn racetrack
der Rentner senior citizen
reparieren v fix; ~ repair
reservieren v reserve
die Reservierung reservation
der Reservierungsschalter reservation desk
das Restaurant restaurant
der Rettungsschwimmer lifeguard
das Rezept prescription
die Rezeption reception
die Richtung direction
der Ring n ring
die Rippe rib (body part)

der Rock skirt
der Rollstuhl wheelchair
die Rollstuhlrampe wheelchair ramp
die Rolltreppe escalator
romantisch romantic
rosa *adj* pink
rot *adj* red
die Route route
der Rücken *n* back (body part)
die Rückenschmerzen backache
der Rucksack backpack
das Ruderboot rowboat
das Rugby rugby
die Ruine ruin

S

der Safe *n* safe (for valuables)
die Sandalen sandals
sauber *adj* clean
die Sauerstoffbehandlung oxygen treatment
die Saugglocke plunger
die Sauna sauna
der Scanner scanner
die Schachtel *n* pack; **~ Zigaretten** pack of cigarettes
der Schal scarf
scharf hot (spicy); **~ sharp**
das Schaufenster window case
der Scheck *n* check [cheque BE] (payment)
die Schere scissors

schicken send; **per Post ~** mail
das Schlachtfeld battleground
schlafen *v* sleep
die Schläfrigkeit drowsiness
der Schlafsack sleeping bag
die Schlafstörung insomnia
der Schlafwagen sleeper [sleeping BE] car
der Schläger racket (sports)
schlecht nauseous; **~ bad**
der Schlepplift drag lift
schließen *v* close (a shop)
das Schließfach locker
das Schloss castle; **~ lock**
die Schlucht ravine
der Schlüssel key; **~ring** key ring
die Schlüsselkarte key card
der Schmerz pain; **Schmerzen haben** be in pain
der Schmuck jewelry
schmutzig dirty
der Schneeschuh snowshoe
schneiden *v* cut
schnell fast
der Schnellzug express train
der Schnitt *n* cut (injury)
der Schnuller pacifier [soother BE]

schön nice; **~ beautiful**
schrecklich terrible
schreiben write
der Schrein shrine
der Schuh shoe
das Schuhgeschäft shoe store
die Schule school
die Schulter shoulder
die Schüssel bowl
schwanger pregnant
schwarz *adj* black
die Schwellung swelling
die Schwester sister
schwierig difficult
das Schwimmbad swimming pool
schwimmen *v* swim
die Schwimmweste life jacket
schwindelig dizzy
schwul *adj* gay
die Schwulenbar gay bar
der Schwulenclub gay club
der See lake
sehbehindert visually impaired
sehen *v* look; **~ see**
die Sehenswürdigkeit attraction
die Seide silk
die Seife *n* soap
die Seilbahn cable car
sein *v* be
die Selbstbedienung self-service
selten rare
seltsam strange
das Seminar seminar
senden *v* send
die Serviette napkin
der Sessellift chair lift

sexuell übertragbare Krankheit sexually transmitted disease (STD)
das Shampoo *n* shampoo
sich scheiden lassen *v* divorce
sicher *adj* safe (protected)
die Sicherheit security
das Sieb colander
das Sightseeing sightseeing
das Silber *n* silver
sitzen *v* sit
der Ski *n* ski
Ski fahren *v* ski
der Skilift ski lift
der Slip briefs (clothing)
die SMS SMS; **eine SMS schicken** *v* text (message)
das Snowboard *n* snowboard
die Socke sock
die Sonne *n* sun
der Sonnenbrand sunburn
die Sonnenbrille sunglasses
die Sonnencreme sunscreen
der Sonnenstich sunstroke
sonnig sunny
das Souvenir souvenir; **~geschäft** souvenir store
das Sparkonto savings (account)
spät late (time)
der Spatel spatula
später later

spazieren gehen v walk

der Spaziergang n walk

die Speicherkarte memory card

speichern v save (computer)

die Speisekarte menu

der Spezialist specialist (doctor)

das Spiel game; ~ match

spielen v play

die Spielhalle arcade

der Spielplatz playground

das Spielzeug toy

der Spielzeugladen toy store

das Spirituosengeschäft liquor store [off-licence BE]

die Spitze lace (fabric)

der Sport sports

die Sportmassage sports massage

das Sportgeschäft sporting goods store

sprechen v speak

der Springbrunnen fountain

die Spülung conditioner (hair)

die Stäbchen chopsticks

das Stadion stadium

die Stadt city; ~ town

der Stadtplan town map

die Stadtrundfahrt sightseeing tour

das Stadtzentrum downtown area

die Stange carton (of cigarettes)

die Statue statue

der Staubsauger vacuum cleaner

das Steakhouse steakhouse

die Steckdose electric outlet

stehlen v steal

steil steep

das Sterlingsilber sterling silver

der Stich n sting

die Stiefel boots

der Stift pen

stillen breastfeed

die Stöcke poles (skiing)

stornieren v cancel

die Strafe n fee (fee for breaking law)

die Strähnchen highlights (hair)

der Strand beach

die Straßenkarte road map

der Strom electricity

die Strumpfhose pantyhose [tights BE]

das Stück n piece; ~ play (theater); ~ slice

der Student student

studieren v study

der Stuhl chair

der Stuhlgang stool (bowel movement)

die Stunde hour

der Süden n south

das Super super (fuel)

der Supermarkt supermarket

das Surfboard surfboard

das Surfbrett windsurfer (board)

süß cute; ~ sweet (taste)

die Süßigkeit candy [sweet BE]

das Sweatshirt sweatshirt

die Synagoge synagogue

synchronisiert dubbed

T

der Tabakhändler tobacconist

die Tablette tablet (medicine)

der Tag day

Tages- one-day (ticket)

das Tal valley

der Tampon tampon

tanken v fill (car)

die Tankstelle gas [petrol BE] station

der Tanzclub dance club

tanzen v dance

die Tasche bag; ~ pocket

die Tasse n cup

taub adj deaf

die Tauchausrüstung diving equipment

tauchen v dive

das Taxi taxi

das Team team

der Teelöffel teaspoon

der Teich pond

das Teil part (for car)

das Telefon n phone

das schnurlose Telefon wireless phone

der Telefonanruf phone call

die Telefonkarte phone card

die Telefonnummer phone number

der Teller plate

der Tempel temple (religious)

das Tennis tennis

der Termin appointment

der Terminal terminal (airport)

teuer expensive

der Text n text

das Theater theater

tief deep

die Tiefkühlkost frozen food

das Tier animal

der Tisch table

die Toilette restroom [toilet BE]

das Toilettenpapier toilet paper

der Topf n pot

die Töpferwaren pottery (pots)

die Tour n tour

der Tourist tourist

traditionell traditional

traurig sad

treffen meet

das Treffen meeting

trennen disconnect (computer)

die Treppe stairs

trinken v drink

das Trinkwasser drinking water

der Tropfen n drop (medicine)

das T-Shirt T-shirt

die Tür door

der Turm tower

die Turnschuhe sneaker

U

die U-Bahn subway [underground BE]

die U-Bahn-Haltestelle subway [underground BE] station

über *prep* over; ~ **Nacht** overnight; **~fallen** *v* mug

die Übergröße plus size

überhitzen overheat (car)

übersetzen translate

überweisen *v* transfer (money)

um (die Ecke) around (the corner)

umändern alter

umarmen *v* hug

die Umkleidekabine fitting room

der Umschlag envelope

umsteigen *v* change (buses); **~** *v* transfer (change trains/flights)

umtauschen *v* exchange (money)

umwerfend stunning

unbeaufsichtigt unattended

der Unfall accident

die Universität university

die Unterhaltung entertainment (amusement)

die Unterhose underwear (underpants BE)

die Unterkunft accommodation

die Unterlegplane groundcloth

unterschreiben *v* sign

der Untertitel *n* subtitle

die Unterwäsche underwear

der Urin urine

der Urlaub vacation [BE holiday]

V

die Vagina vagina

vaginal vaginal; **die ~e Entzündung** vaginal infection

der Vater father

der V-Ausschnitt V-neck

der Veganer *n* vegan

der Vegetarier *n* vegetarian

der Ventilator fan (appliance)

verbieten *v* prohibit

verbinden *v* connect (internet)

die Verbindung connection

die Vereinigten Staaten United States (U.S.)

verfügbar available

vergewaltigen *v* rape

die Vergewaltigung *n* rape

der Vergnügungspark amusement park

verheiratet married

verkaufen *v* sell

verlangen *v* charge (cost)

verlieren *v* lose (something)

verlobt engaged

verloren lost

verschlucken *v* swallow

verschneit snowy

verschreiben *v* prescribe (medication)

versenden *v* ship

die Versicherung insurance

die Versicherungsgesellschaft insurance company

die Versicherungskarte insurance card

die Verstauchung *n* sprain

verstehen understand

die Verstopfung constipation

verwitwet widowed

verzögern *v* delay

viel much; **~ a lot**; **~en Dank** thank you; **wie ~** how much

violett *adj* purple

die Visitenkarte business card

das Visum visa

das Vitamin vitamin

die Vitrine display case

der Vogel bird

die Volksmusik folk music

das Volleyballspiel volleyball game

Vollzeit- full-time

vor before; **Viertel ~ vier** a quarter to four

die Vorfahrt right of way

die Vorhersage *n* forecast

die Vorspeise appetizer [starter BE]

vorstellen *v* introduce (person)

vorübergehend temporary

W

wählen *v* dial

während during

die Währung currency

der Währungsumtausch currency exchange

der Wald forest

die Wanderroute walking route

die Wanderschuhe hiking boots

die Wanduhr wall clock

wann when (time)

die Ware *n* good; **~** product

die Waren goods

warm *adj* warm (temperature)

warten wait

der Warteraum waiting room

die Wartezeit *n* waiting period

was what

das Waschbecken *n* sink

die Wäscherei laundry (facility)

der Wäscheservice laundry service

die Waschmaschine washing machine

waschmaschinenfest machine washable

das Waschmittel detergent

der Waschsalon laundromat [launderette BE]

der Wasserfall
waterfall

die Wasserski water
skis

das Wechselgeld *n*
change (money)

der Wechselkurs
exchange rate

wechseln *v* change

die Wechselstube
currency exchange
office

wecken *v* wake

der Weckruf wake-up
call

weich soft

das Weingut vineyard

die Weinkarte wine list

weiß *adj* white

das Weißgold white
gold

weit *adv* far (distance);
~ *adj* loose (fit)

weitsichtig far (long
BE)- sighted

das Wellness-Center
spa

wenig *adj* little (not
much)

weniger less

wer who

der Wert value

wertvoll valuable

der Westen *n* west

das Wetter weather

wickeln *v* change
(baby)

wie how; ~ **viel** how
much

wiederholen repeat

willkommen *adj*
welcome

die Windel diaper
[nappy BE]

die Wirbelsäule spine
(body part)

wireless wireless

wo where

die Woche week

das Wochenende
weekend

wöchentlich weekly

der Wohnwagen
mobile home

die Wolle wool

wunder schön
beautiful

die Wüste *n* desert

Z

der Zahn tooth

der Zahnarzt dentist

die Zahnpaste
toothpaste

der Zeh *n* toe

der Zehennagel toenail

das Zeichen symbol
(keyboard)

zeigen *v* show (somebody something)

die Zeit time

der Zeitraum period
(of time)

die Zeitung newspaper

der Zeitungskiosk
newsstand

das Zelt tent

der Zelthering tent
peg

die Zeltstange tent
pole

der Zentimeter
centimeter

zerbrochen broken
(smashed)

das Zertifikat
certificate

ziehen *v* extract (tooth);
~ *v* pull (door sign)

die Zigarette
cigarette

die Zigarre cigar

das Zimmer room

der Zimmerschlüssel
room key

der Zimmerservice
room service

das Zinn pewter

der Zoll customs;
~ duty (tax)

zollfrei duty-free

der Zoo zoo

zu *adv* too; ~ *prep* to

der Zug train

die Zunge tongue

zurückgeben *v* return
(something)

der Zutritt *n* access

INDEX

Alter Markt square 44
Altstadt (Old Town) 10, 36

Berchtesgaden, Germany 70

Capuchin Monastery 59
Castle Hohenwerfen, Werfen 74
Cathedral 39
Cathedral Museum 40
children 94
Church of St Sebastian 52
Collegiate Church 46

Durrnberg Salt Mines, Hallein 73

Eisriesenwelt ice caves 75

Festivals 86, 95
Festspielhauser (Festival Halls) 46
Festung Hohensalzburg 30
Folklore Museum 64
Franciscan Church 48
Fuschlsee lake 80

Getreidegasse street 44, 90

Grossglockner High Alpine Road 76

Hallein 72
Hangar-7 61
Haus der Natur 49
Hellbrunn Palace and Gardens 62

Kajetanerkirche St Maximilian church 35
Kapitelplatz 42
Kapuzinerberg 59
Kehlsteinhaus (Eagle's Nest), Germany 70
Klessheim Palace 65
Konigssee lake 71
Krimml Waterfalls 78

Landestheater (Regional Theatre) 55
Leopoldskron Palace 60
Linzergasse 52

Makartplatz 53
Marionettentheater (Puppet Theatre) 55
markets 90
Mirabell Gardens 57
Mirabell Palace 57
Monchsberg 29
Mondsee lake 83
Mozart Dinner Concert 89
Mozartplatz 42

Mozart's Birthplace 45
Mozart's Residence 54
Mozart, Wolfgang Amadeus 23, 41, 44, 81
Mulln Monastery 51
Museum der Moderne 50

Nightlife 89
Nonnberg Benedictine Convent 33

Obersalzburg, Germany 70
Open-Air Museum, Grossgmain 69

Panorama Museum 39
Pfahlbaumuseum, Mondsee 83

Residenz 37
Residenzplatz 36
Rupertinum gallery 48

Salt Mines, Germany 71
Salzburg Card 12
Salzburg Museum 38
Salzburg Zoo 64
Salzkammergut 79
Shopping 89
Silent Night Museum, Hallein 74
Spielzeugmuseum (Toy Museum) 50

Sports 91
St Bartholoma, Konigssee 72
St Erhard im Nonntal church 35
St Gilgen village 81

Stiegl's Brauwelt 62
Stiftskeller St Peter church 41
Stiftung Mozarteum 55
St Mark's Church 49
St Peter's Abbey 41

St Wolfgang village 82

Untersberg mountain 67

Werfen 74

Berlitz pocket guide

SALZBURG

Fifth Edition 2018

Editor: Sîan Marsh
Author: Trudie Trox
Head of Production: Rebeka Davies
Picture Editor: Tom Smyth
Cartography Update: Carte
Update Production: Apa Digital
Photography Credits: Apa Publications 5M; Austrian National Tourist Office 6L, 6R, 7L, 15, 17, 19, 22, 84, 92, 96, 99, 100; Britta Jaschinski/Apa Publications 4MC, 5MC, 7R, 21, 42, 50, 58, 69, 72, 73, 76, 78, 80, 81, 83, 103, 104; davelogan/iStockphoto 45; donstock/iStockphoto 13; Getty Images 1, 25, 47, 90; iStock 5TC, 5MC, 5M, 28, 31, 32, 37, 40, 46, 48, 57, 71; joachimberger/Fotolia 4TC, 38; magann/Fotolia 34; Matthias Kabel 66; Mockford & Bonetti/Apa Publications 64; Mozarteum 55; Natalia Bratslavsky/iStockphoto 53; Nataliia Fedori/iStockphoto 30; repistu/iStockphoto 5T, 63, 67; Sven Brenner/Fotolia 11; Tobboo/Fotolia 4TL, 74; Tourismus Salzburg 4ML, 87, 88; Ulrich Grill/Redbull 61
Cover Picture: iStock

Distribution
UK, Ireland and Europe: Apa Publications (UK) Ltd; sales@insightguides.com
United States and Canada: Ingram Publisher Services; ips@ingramcontent.com
Australia and New Zealand: Woodslane; info@woodslane.com.au
Southeast Asia: Apa Publications (SN) Pte; singaporeoffice@insightguides.com
Worldwide: Apa Publications (UK) Ltd; sales@insightguides.com

Special Sales, Content Licensing and CoPublishing
Insight Guides can be purchased in bulk quantities at discounted prices. We can create special editions, personalised jackets and corporate imprints tailored to your needs. sales@insightguides.com; www.insightguides.biz

Contact us
Every effort has been made to provide accurate information in this publication, but changes are inevitable. The publisher cannot be responsible for any resulting loss, inconvenience or injury. We would appreciate it if readers would call our attention to any errors or outdated information. We also welcome your suggestions; please contact us at: berlitz@apaguide.co.uk
www.insightguides.com/berlitz